LAW & MENTAL HEALTH PROFESSIONALS

MASSACHUSETTS

LAW & MENTAL HEALTH PROFESSIONALS SERIES

Bruce D. Sales and Michael O. Miller, Series Editors

ARIZONA: Miller and Sales
MASSACHUSETTS: Brant
NEW JERSEY: Wulach
TEXAS: Shuman

LAW & MENTAL HEALTH PROFESSIONALS

MASSACHUSETTS

Jonathan Brant

AMERICAN PSYCHOLOGICAL ASSOCIATION
Washington, DC

Published by
American Psychological Association
1200 Seventeenth Street, NW
Washington, DC 20036

Copies may be ordered from
APA Order Department
P.O. Box 2710
Hyattsville, MD 20784

Text and cover design by Rubin Krassner, Silver Spring, MD
Composition by TAPSCO, Inc., Akron, PA
Printing by Edwards Brothers, Inc., Ann Arbor, MI
Technical editing by Allison Rottmann
Production coordination by Susan Bedford

Library of Congress Cataloging-in-Publication Data

Brant, Jonathan.
    Law & mental health professionals. Massachusetts/Jonathan
Brant.
        p.   cm.
    Includes bibliographical references and index.
    ISBN 1-55798-124-8
    1. Mental health personnel—Legal status, laws, etc.—
Massachusetts.   2. Forensic psychiatry—Massachusetts.
3. Psychology, Forensic.   I. Title.   II. Title: Law and mental
health professionals. Massachusetts.
    KFM2726.5.P73B73   1991
    344.744′044—dc20
    [347.440444]   91-22854
                                                          CIP

Printed in the United States of America
First Edition

Contents

Acknowledgments

I wish to thank the editors of the Law & Mental Health Professionals series, Bruce D. Sales and Michael O. Miller, for inviting me to write the Massachusetts volume. Paul Appelbaum suggested me to the editors and encouraged me to take on this task.

The following persons reviewed all or part of the manuscript: Doris Magwood, Alexander Greer, Eric Harris, Gerald Koocher, Stan Goldman, and Gretchen Graef. They all improved the quality of this work with their comments and encouragement. Any remaining errors are my fault.

Dolores R. Millard typed the manuscript.

Renee Tankenoff Brant offered helpful comments.

Simone Brant and Justin Brant contributed nothing at all to this book but will appreciate seeing their names in print.

Editors' Preface

The Need to Know the Law

For years, providers of mental health services (hereinafter mental health professionals or MHPs) have been directly affected by the law. At one end of the continuum, their practice has been controlled by laws covering such matters as licensure and certification, third-party reimbursement, and professional incorporation. At the other end, they have been courted by the legal system to aid in its administration, providing such services as evaluating the mental status of litigants, providing expert testimony in court, and engaging in therapy with court-referred juveniles and adults. Even when not directly affected, MHPs find themselves indirectly affected by the law since their clients sometimes become involved in legal entanglements that involve mental status issues (e.g., divorce proceedings or termination of parental rights hearings).

Despite this pervasive influence, most professionals do not know about, much less understand, most of the laws that affect their practice, the services they render, and the clients they serve. This state of affairs is particularly troubling for several reasons. First, not knowing about the laws that affect one's practice typically results in the MHP's not gaining the benefits that the law may provide. Consider the law relating to the incorporation of professionals. It confers significant benefit, but only if it is known about and applied. The fact that it has been enacted by the state legislature does not help the MHP, any more than an MHP will be of help to a distressed person who refuses to contact the MHP.

Second, not knowing about the laws that affect the services they render can result in incompetent performance of, and liability for, the MHP either through the civil law (e.g., malpractice law) or through criminal sanctions. A brief example may help underscore this point. When an MHP is asked to evaluate a party to a lawsuit and testify in court, the court (the law's term for the judge) is asking the professional to assess and testify about whether that litigant meets some legal standard. The court is often not concerned with the defendant's mental health per se, although this may be relevant to the MHP's evaluation of the person. Rather, the court wants to know if the person meets the legal standard as it is set down by the law. Not knowing the legal standard means that the MHP is most likely evaluating the person for the wrong goal and providing the court with irrelevant information, at least from the court's point of view. Regretfully, we personally know of too many cases in which this has occurred.

Third, not knowing the law that affects the clients that MHPs serve may significantly diminish their capability for handling their clients' distress. For example, a client who is undergoing a divorce and child custody dispute may have distorted beliefs about what may happen during the legal proceedings. A basic understanding of the controlling law in this area will allow the therapist to be more sensitive in rendering therapy.

The Problem in Accessing Legal Information

Given the need for this information, why have MHPs not systematically sought it out? Part of the reason lies in the concern over their ability to understand legal doctrines. Indeed, this is a legitimate worry, especially if they had to read original legal materials that were not collected, organized, and described with an MHP audience in mind. This is of particular concern since laws are written in terms and phrases of "art" that do not always share the common lay definition or usage, while some terms and phrases are left ambiguous and undefined or are used differently for different legal topics. Another part of the reason is that the law affecting MHPs and their clients is not readily available—even to lawyers. There are no compendiums that identify the topics that these laws cover or present an analysis of each topic for easy reference.

To compound the difficulty, the law does not treat the different mental health professional disciplines uniformly or always specify the particular disciplines as being covered by it. Nor does the law emanate from a single legal forum. Each state enacts its own rules and regulations, often resulting in wide variations in the way a topic is handled across the United States. Multiply this confusion times the one hundred or so topics that relate to mental health practice. In addition, the law within a state does not come from one legal source. Rather, there are five primary ones: the state constitution; state legislative enactments (statutes); state agency administrative rules and regulations; rules of court promulgated by the state supreme court; and state and federal court cases that apply, interpret, and construe this existing state law. To know about one of these sources without knowing how its pronouncements on a given topic have been modified by these other sources can result in one's making erroneous conclusions about the operation of the law. Finally, mental health practice also comes under the purview of federal law (constitutional and statutory law, administrative rules and regulations, and case law). Federal law authorizes direct payments to MHPs for their services to some clients, sets standards for delivery of services in federal facilities (e.g., Veterans

Administration Hospitals), and articulates the law that guides cases that are tried in federal courts under federal law.

Purposes of This Series

What is needed, therefore, is a book for each state, the District of Columbia, and the federal jurisdictions that comprehensively and accurately reviews and integrates all of the laws that affect MHPs in that jurisdiction (hereinafter state). To ensure currency, regular supplements to these books will be drafted. These materials will be written so that they are completely understandable to MHPs, as well as to lawyers. In order to accomplish these goals, we have tried to identify every legal topic that affects mental health practice, making each one the subject of a chapter. Each chapter, in turn, will describe the legal standards that the MHP will be operating under and the relevant legal process that the MHP will be operating within. If a state does not have relevant law on this issue, then a brief explanation of how this law works in other states will be presented while noting the lack of regulation in this area within the state under consideration.

This type of coverage facilitates other purposes of the series. Although each chapter will be written in order to state exactly what is the present state of the law and not argue for or against any particular approach, we hope that the comprehensiveness of the coverage will encourage MHPs to question the desirability of their states' approach to each topic. Such information and concern should provide the impetus for initiating legislation and litigation on the part of state mental health associations to ensure that the law reflects scientific knowledge and professional values to the greatest extent possible.

In some measure, states will initially be hampered in this proactivity since they will not know what legal alternatives are available and how desirable each alternative actually is. When a significant number of books in this series is available, however, it will allow for nationally oriented policy studies to identify the variety of legal approaches that are currently in use and to assess the validity of the behavioral assumptions underlying each variant, and ultimately lead to a conclusion as to the relative desirability of alternate approaches.[1] Thus, two other purposes of this book are to foster comprehensive analyses of the laws affecting MHPs across all states and the validity of the behavioral assumptions underlying these laws, and to promote political, legislative, and

---

1. Sales, B. D. (1983). The legal regulation of psychology: Professional and scientific interactions. In C. J. Scheirer & B. L. Hammonds (Eds.), *The master lecture series: Vol. 2: Psychology and law* (pp. 5–36). Washington, DC: American Psychological Association.

legal action to change laws that are inappropriate and impede the effective delivery of services. Legal change may be required because of gaps in legal regulation, overregulation, and regulation based on invalid behavioral and social assumptions. We hope this process will increase the rationality of future laws in this area and improve the effectiveness and quality of mental health service delivery nationally.

There are three remaining purposes for this series. First, although it will *not* replace the need for legal counsel, this series will make the MHP an intelligent consumer of legal services. This ability is gaining importance in an era of increasing professionalization and litigiousness. Second, it will ensure that MHPs are aware of the law's mandates when providing expert services (e.g., evaluation and testimony) within the legal system. Although chapters will not address how to clinically assess for the legal standard, provider competency will increase since providers now will be sure of the goals of their service (e.g., the legal standard that they are to assess for) as well as their roles and responsibilities within the legal system as to the particular topic in issue. Third and finally, each book will make clear that the legal standards that MHPs are asked to assess for by the law have typically not been translated into behavioral correlates. Nor are there discussions of tests, scales, and procedures for MHPs to use in assessing for the behavioral correlates of the legal standards in most cases. This series will provide the impetus for such research and writing.

Content and Organization of Volumes

Each book in this series is organized into six sections. Section 1 addresses the legal credentialing of MHPs. Section 2 deals with the different business forms for conducting one's practice. Section 3 addresses insurance reimbursement and tax deductions that clients can receive for utilizing mental health services. With the business matters covered, the book then turns to the law directly affecting service delivery. Section 4 starts by covering the law that affects the maintenance and privacy of professional information. Section 5 considers each area of law that may require the services of MHPs. It is subdivided into five parts: families and juveniles, other civil matters, topics that apply similarly in both civil and criminal cases, criminal matters, and voluntary and involuntary receipt of state services by the clients of mental health services. The last section of the book, Section 6, discusses the law that limits service delivery and sets liability for unethical and illegal behavior as a service provider.

Collectively, the chapters in these sections represent all topics pertaining to the law as it affects MHPs in their practices. Two caveats are in order, however. First, the law changes slowly over time. Thus, a supplement service will update all chapters on a regular basis. Second, as MHPs become more involved in the legal system, new opportunities for involvement are likely to arise. To be responsive to these developments, the supplements also will contain additional chapters reflecting these new roles and responsibilities.

Some final points about the content of the books are in order. The exact terms that the law chooses are used even if they are a poor choice from an MHP's point of view. And where terms are defined by the law, that information is presented. The reader may be frustrated, however, because as has already been noted, the law does not always define terms or provide detailed guidance. This does not mean that legal words and phrases can be taken lightly. The law sets the rules that MHPs and their clients must operate by; thus, chapters must be read carefully. This should not be too arduous a task since most chapters are relatively short. On the other hand, such brevity will leave some readers frustrated because chapters appear not to go far enough in answering their questions. Note that all the law in a state is covered in the relevant volume. If there is no law, however, there is no coverage. If a question is not answered in the text it is because law in that state has not addressed the issue. Relatedly, if an obligation or benefit is created by a professional regulation (i.e., a rule of a professional organization) but is not directly recognized by the law, it is not covered. Thus, for example, professional credentials are not addressed in these volumes.

Finally, we want to point out that in some instances, the pronoun "he" is used generically to refer to both sexes. Most notably, the pronoun is used when quoting directly from the law. Legal language is generally consistent in its preference for using the masculine form of the pronoun; it is not always feasible to attempt a rewording.

Bruce D. Sales
Michael O. Miller
Series Editors

Author's Preface

This book is principally a treatment of state law applicable to MHPs. A comprehensive treatment of federal law, which is also relevant to the actions of MHPs, is beyond the scope of this work as it would expand it by volumes or require a more limited treatment of each subject. The sources of state law treated in this work include the state constitution, state statutes, state administrative rules, state judicial decisions, and state judicial rules.

The Massachusetts Constitution, which was adopted in 1780 and served as the model for the Constitution of the United States, establishes the framework for state government and declares important individual rights. Citations to the Massachusetts Constitution appear in the following form: Mass. Const. art. 1. This reference indicates that this citation is to a section of the Massachusetts Constitution that can be found in the bound volumes of Massachusetts statutes and constitutional provisions, in the volume that is marked *Constitution* and contains article 1 of the constitution.

Citations to state statutes, which result from legislation passed by the Massachusetts General Court (the collective name for the House of Representatives and Senate) and signed into law by the governor, appear in the following form: Mass. Gen. L. ch. 123, § 10. This particular citation is a reference to the bound volumes of statutes labeled *Massachusetts General Laws Annotated, Annotated Laws of Massachusetts,* or *Massachusetts General Laws Official Edition.* The specific number refers to section 10 of chapter 123 in those volumes.

These compilations of statutes, except in the *Massachusetts General Laws Official Edition,* contain additional useful material. The compilers attempt to include citations and summaries of reported cases that discuss the statute or constitutional provision in question. Thus, one may use these case references, called *annotations,* to begin research on how the statute or constitutional provision has been interpreted by the courts. The compilations also contain references to prior statutes that have been repealed. A review of these repealed statutes may be necessary to understand an earlier judicial opinion interpreting them or to resolve an ambiguity in the intent of the legislature in changing the statute.

State administrative rules are created by state agencies operating under the authority delegated to them by the legislature to carry out specific agency functions. For example, the legislation creating the Massachusetts Board of Registration of Psychologists does not create a code of ethics for psychologists, but gives the Board the authority to make administrative rules creating a code of ethics for psychologists. These rules do not appear in the statute books; instead, they are kept in a series entitled *Code of Massachusetts Regulations (CMR)*. References to the administrative code appear in the following form: 110 CMR 3.07. The administrative rule referred to by this citation can be found in the volume of the series containing chapter 110. The specific regulation is 3.07.

State judicial decisions are the product of judge-made law. Reported decisions are those of the two appellate courts, the Supreme Judicial Court of Massachusetts and the Massachusetts Appeals Court. Citations to these decisions appear in two official reporters, the *Massachusetts Reports* for the Supreme Judicial Court and the *Massachusetts Appeals Court Reports* for the Appeals Court. State judicial decisions can also be found in an unofficial reporter known as the *Northeast Reporter*. Thus, a decision of the Supreme Judicial Court would be cited as 404 Mass. 231, 537 N.E.2d 1241 (1989). This would indicate that the case is reported at page 231 of volume 404 of the *Massachusetts Reports* and at page 1241 of volume 537 of the second series of the *Northeast Reporter* and that the case is from 1989.

State judicial rules, as contrasted with judicial decisions, are rules adopted by the courts which govern the procedure for cases. Rules cited in this volume include the Massachusetts Rules of Civil Procedure, the Massachusetts Rules of Criminal Procedure, and the Massachusetts Rules of Domestic Relations Procedure.

Although the focus of this work is on state rather than federal law applicable to MHPs in Massachusetts, occasional reference is necessary to federal decisions interpreting or limiting state law. The citations to these federal decisions are from the United States District Court (F. Supp.), the United States Court of Appeals (F. or F. 2d), and the United States Supreme Court (U.S., S. Ct., or L. Ed.). As is the case with the reports of state decisions, the number preceding the reporter is the volume, and the number following is the page. References to federal legislation appear in the form 26 U.S.C. Sec. 213 (a) (1987). This particular citation to the United States Code, the repository of federal legislation, is from title 26, section 213 (a), current as of 1987. In addition, there are citations to treatises and law review articles. These references may provide a fuller background on an issue of interest to MHPs.

Finally, although some chapters were updated until the manuscript went to press, the reader should consider the entire volume current as of April 1, 1991.

Jonathan Brant

Legal Credentialing

Licensure and Regulation of Psychiatrists

The licensure and regulation of psychiatrists is governed by the statute that establishes the Board of Registration in Medicine, sets qualifications and procedures for licensure of physicians, regulates the conduct of physicians, and prescribes sanctions for violations of the statute.[1] There is no separate licensure provision pertaining to the practice of psychiatry. Psychiatrists are licensed as physicians and obtain specialized certification through the National Board of Psychiatry and Neurology.

Board of Registration in Medicine

The Board of Registration in Medicine (Board) under the Division of Registration in the Executive Office of Consumer Affairs and Business Regulation is the state agency that licenses and regulates psychiatrists.[2] It consists of seven members appointed by the governor for 3-year terms. The Board is composed of two citizens and five actively practicing physicians. It is responsible for determining eligibility for licensure of physicians and for regulating the professional conduct of licensed physicians.[3]

Licensure

An applicant will be licensed to practice medicine in Massachusetts if he or she:

---

1. Mass. Gen. L. ch. 112, §§ 1–12.
2. Mass. Gen. L. ch. 13, § 10.
3. Mass. Gen. L. ch. 112, § 5.

1. graduated from a legally charted medical school in the United States or Canada or the equivalent;[4]
2. successfully completed an approved[5] 12-month hospital internship, residency, or fellowship program or hold a full-time academic appointment in a medical school in Massachusetts;
3. possess the physical and mental capability to safely engage in the practice of medicine;
4. committed no prior acts that would constitute grounds for disciplinary action (see subsequent text on disciplinary action);
5. never had a medical license refused, revoked, suspended, or restricted because of any activity related to their inability to competently and safely practice medicine; and
6. passed a written examination administered by the Board or the equivalent national committee.[6]

A graduate of an approved foreign school of medicine may be licensed if he or she can meet the preceding basic requirements; read, write, speak, understand, and be understood in English; holds a standard certificate issued by the Education Council for Foreign Medical Graduates; and has completed an additional 12-month internship, residency, or fellowship.[7]

A limited license to practice medicine in a hospital under supervision may be granted to a person who is otherwise qualified as an applicant but is a foreign medical graduate without the standard permanent resident certificate, or to a person who is completing an internship or residency.[8]

Exceptions to Licensing

The licensing law does not apply to persons providing emergency medical assistance; persons undertaking an approved internship, residency, or fellowship; medical officers in the armed forces, Veterans Administration, or Public Health Service; physicians licensed and residing outside of Massachusetts who consult with a Massachusetts licensed physician; and physicians who are invited to Massachusetts by an approved school of medicine for the sole purpose of promoting professional education and who do not see patients in Massachusetts.[9]

---

4. Mass. Gen. L. ch. 112, § 2.
5. Approved by the American Medical Association or the Association of Canadian Medical Colleges. Mass. Gen. L. ch. 112, § 2.
6. Most registrants substitute passage of the national examination of the National Board of Medical Examiners for this requirement. Mass. Gen. L. ch. 112, § 2.
7. Mass. Gen. L. ch. 112, § 2.
8. Mass. Gen. L. ch. 112, § 9.
9. Mass. Gen. L. ch. 112, § 2; 243 CMR 1.00. et seq.

Regulation

Disciplinary Actions Against a Licensed Physician

Licenses are issued for 2-year periods and are renewed on the birthday of the registrant.[10] The Board requires an applicant for registration or renewal to demonstrate that he or she is carrying adequate medical malpractice insurance.[11]

The disciplinary unit of the Board of Regulation in Medicine is responsible for investigating complaints about physicians.[12] The Board also has a risk-management unit designed to assist physicians in avoiding malpractice. The Board requires each physician to complete a risk management course as part of continuing education requirements for renewal of a license.[13] All disciplinary actions taken by hospitals or professional associations or settlements or judgments against physicians in malpractice actions must be reported to the Board.[14]

The Board may revoke a physician's license if the physician:[15]

1. fraudulently procured the license,

2. committed a criminal offense relating to the practice of medicine,

3. practiced medicine while under the influence of drugs or while suffering from a physical or mental disability,

4. used controlled substances or prescription-only drugs outside of a course of treatment,

5. provided any controlled substance or prescription-only drug for other than accepted therapeutic purposes, or

6. was found guilty of a criminal offense calling into question the ability to practice medicine.

Investigation by the Board

The Board sets priorities concerning investigation of complaints and determines how to proceed.[16] Matters under investigation are confidential until the investigation is complete.[17] The Board may subpoena records and other materials during the course of its investigation.[18]

---

10. Mass. Gen. L. ch. 112, § 2.
11. Mass. Gen. L. ch. 112, § 5.
12. *Id.*
13. *Id.*
14. Mass. Gen. L. ch. 112, §§ 5B and 5E.
15. Mass. Gen. L. ch. 112, § 5.
16. Mass. Gen. L. ch. 112, § 5K.
17. Mass. Gen. L. ch. 112, § 5.
18. *Id.*

Generally, conviction of a criminal offense relating to the practice of medicine will lead to revocation of license.[19] If the Board's investigation reveals possible criminal conduct, the Board may report the matter to a district attorney for possible prosecution.[20] Violations may also form the basis for a civil suit against a psychiatrist. (See Chapters 6.5 and 6.6.)

The Board's investigatory unit investigates consumer complaints against physicians.[21] Most complaints are dismissed at this stage. When the Board believes that the conduct of a physician should be grounds for discipline, it will issue a Statement of Allegations, which is a formal accusation. After the physician responds, a hearing officer employed by the Division of Administrative Law Appeals will conduct a hearing by taking testimony. The hearing officer will write a tentative decision recommending a course of action to the Board. The hearing officer, as the person who hears the actual testimony, is the judge of the witness' testimony.[22] The Board issues the ultimate decision, which may include sanctions such as fines, revocation of license, suspension, or reprimand. A physician who is disciplined may appeal the Board's decision to the courts.[23] The Supreme Judicial Court has original jurisdiction over appeals from decisions of the Board.[24]

---

19. Levy v. Board of Registration and Discipline in Medicine, 378 Mass. 519, 392 N.E.2d 1036 (1979).
20. Mass. Gen. L. ch. 112, § 5.
21. 243 CMR 1.03 (3).
22. Morris v. Board of Registration in Medicine, 405 Mass. 103, 539 N.E.2d 50 (1989).
23. Hellman v. Board of Registration in Medicine, 404 Mass. 800, 537 N.E.2d 150 (1989).
24. Mass. Gen. L. ch. 112, § 64.

1.2

Licensure and Regulation of Psychiatric Nurses

The licensure and regulation of psychiatric nurses are governed by statutes[1] that establish the Board of Registration in Nursing, set qualifications and procedures for licensure of nurses, define the practice of nursing, give exceptions to licensure, and prescribe sanctions for violations of the law. While there is no separate licensure pertaining to the practice of psychiatric nursing, the Board of Registration has guidelines for certifying psychiatric nurses in various categories such as psychiatric nurse, mental health specialist[2] and psychiatric nurse, mental health clinical specialist.[3] Holders of these specialized titles are affected by confidentiality and privilege requirements (see Chapters 4.2 and 4.3).

Board of Registration in Nursing

The Board of Registration in Nursing (Board) is the state agency that licenses and regulates nurses. It consists of eight members appointed by the governor for 6-year terms.[4] The Board is composed of five licensed nurses, one citizen, and two licensed practical nurses. The Board is responsible for licensing and regulating professional nurses and licensed practical nurses.[5]

---

1. Mass. Gen. L. ch. 13, § 13 and ch. 112, § 74.
2. 244 CMR 4.23.
3. 244 CMR 4.26 (3); *see also* Mass. Gen. L. ch. 123, § 1, as amended by St. 1989, ch. 304.
4. Mass. Gen. L. ch. 13, § 13.
5. Mass. Gen. L. ch. 112, §§ 74–81C.

Licensure

An applicant will be licensed as a professional nurse in Massachusetts if he or she has:[6]

1. completed the basic professional curriculum of an approved school of professional nursing, and

2. passed a written exam administered by the Board.

Licenses must be renewed on the birthdate of the registrant on every even numbered year.[7] An applicant for renewal must satisfy the Board's requirements for continuing education.[8]

Exceptions to Licensing

The Board has the discretion to temporarily license nurses licensed in other states who accompany patients to Massachusetts for a period of up to 1 year.[9]

Regulation

Disciplinary Actions Against a Licensed Nurse

A nurse's license may be suspended, revoked, or placed on probationary status for violation of a statute or the regulations of the Board.[10] Unlike the Medicine Board, the Nursing Board does not have its own disciplinary unit. Rather, it depends on the disciplinary unit of the Division of Registration, the state agency of which it is a part. The Board may refer apparent criminal violations to the appropriate district attorney for prosecution.

Investigations by the Board

The Board is charged with investigating complaints against nurses.[11] The procedures for investigation and disciplinary proceedings are the same as the Board of Registration in Medicine.[12]

Penalties for Violations

In addition to administrative penalties such as revocation, probation, supervision, or reprimand,[13] the Board may refer for prose-

---

6. Mass. Gen. L. ch. 112, § 74.
7. *Id.*
8. *Id.*
9. Mass. Gen. L. ch. 112, § 76.
10. Mass. Gen. L. ch. 112, § 77.
11. *Id.*
12. 244 CMR 7.01 *et seq.*
13. 244 CMR 7.08.

cution persons accused of acting as professional or practical nurses without appropriate license.[14] Violations may also form the basis for a civil suit against a nurse. (See Chapters 6.5 and 6.6.)

14. Mass. Gen. L. ch. 112, §§ 80 and 80A.

1.3

Licensure and Regulation of Psychologists

The licensure and regulation of psychologists is governed by a statute that establishes a Board of Registration of Psychologists, defines terms contained within the statute, sets qualifications and procedures for licensure of psychologists, regulates the conduct of licensed psychologists, provides for administrative hearings, states exceptions to licensure, bars the practice of medicine by psychologists, and prescribes sanctions for violations of the chapter.[1]

Board of Registration of Psychologists

The Board of Registration of Psychologists (Board) is the state agency that licenses and regulates psychologists. It consists of nine members appointed by the governor for 5-year terms. The Board is responsible for licensing psychologists and investigating complaints.[2]

Licensure

The statutes and rules pertaining to licensure set out qualifications, fees, examination procedures, and exemptions to the rules.[3] An individual is eligible for licensure if he or she:[4]

---

1. Mass. Gen. L. ch. 13, § 76; see 251 CMR 3.01.
2. Mass. Gen. L. ch. 112, § 128.
3. Mass. Gen. L. ch. 112, § 119.
4. Mass. Gen. L. ch. 112, § 120; see also 251 CMR 3.03–3.04.

1. is of good moral character—generally denoted by the absence of ethical violations or conviction for offenses involving moral turpitude;

2. has received a doctorate degree from an approved program of studies in psychology;

3. has worked as a psychologist for the equivalent of 2 years, including 1 year after receipt of the doctorate; and

4. conducts practice in accordance with established professional standards.

In addition, psychologists must pass an examination established by the Board. This written examination may be waived for persons who have obtained an acceptable score on the nationally administered examination for the Professional Practice of Psychology or have been granted a diploma by the American Board of Professional Psychology.[5]

All licenses are valid for two years, beginning July 1.

The Board may grant a temporary license for a period of up to 1 year to a psychologist licensed to practice in another state.[6]

Specialty Certification: Health Service Provider

A licensed psychologist may obtain certification as a health service provider. The applicant must have 2 years supervised health service experience, of which at least 1 year is postdoctoral and at least 1 year is in a health services training program.[7]

Exceptions to the Regulations

The law does not restrict the activities and services of all persons who call themselves psychologists. Six classes of persons are allowed exemptions. Without complying with the licensure procedures, they may use the title of psychologist in their official capacity as:[8]

1. an employee of an accredited institution of higher education who has obtained a doctorate degree and who uses the title only in conjunction with research activities;

2. a person employed with a salary by a primary or secondary school who is certified to use the title *Certified School Psychologist* by the State Department of Education (see Chapter 1.6);

---

5. Mass. Gen. L. ch. 112, § 121.
6. Mass. Gen. L. ch. 112, § 124.
7. Mass. Gen. L. ch. 112, § 120.
8. Mass. Gen. L. ch. 112, § 123.

3. an employee who works on salary for a government agency;
4. a student in psychology pursuing an official course of graduate study at an approved educational institution; the title used at the institution must contain *psychologist trainee* or *psychologist intern* and can only be used in conjunction with activities that are part of the supervised program;
5. a person eligible for licensure who provides consultative services no more than 1 day per month; and
6. a salaried employee of an educational or nonprofit organization who provides consultation of a research nature.

Regulation

Violations

A psychologist's license may be suspended for up to 2 years, revoked, or placed on probationary status for:[9]

1. conviction of a felony involving moral turpitude in the practice of psychology, such as sexual improprieties with a patient;
2. fraud or deceit in establishing one's qualifications under this chapter; or
3. improper, unethical, or grossly negligent conduct in the practice of psychology.

Penalties for Improperly Claiming to be a Psychologist

Any person who holds him- or herself out to be a psychologist without the required licenses is guilty of a crime that carries a penalty of a fine of up to $500 or up to 3 months imprisonment.[10]

As with the Boards of Medicine and Nursing, the Board of Registration of Psychologists investigates complaints and holds hearings that may lead to restriction or revocation of licensure.[11]

---

9. Mass. Gen. L. ch. 112, § 128.
10. Mass. Gen. L. ch. 112, § 122.
11. 251 CMR 1.00–1.07.

1.4

Subdoctoral and Unlicensed Psychologists

The status of subdoctoral-level psychologists is an important issue, both as pertains to the law and to the practice of psychology. Massachusetts does not permit a person without a doctorate to be licensed as a psychologist.[1] Since the statutory definition of *psychologist* requires receipt of a doctorate, it is a violation of law for a person lacking a doctorate to hold him- or herself out as a psychologist unless one of the exceptions described below applies or the person was licensed before the law was changed to require a doctorate.[2]

Psychologists Exempted From Licensure

As already noted in Chapter 1.3, the law provides that a person must be licensed by the Board of Registration of Psychologists (Board) to use the title *psychologist*. There are exceptions applying to employees as follows:[3]

1. employees of institutions of higher education and research employees of government agencies and nonprofit agencies may use the title of psychologist in conjunction with their academic activities and services;

2. psychologists employed by an elementary or secondary school system as school psychologists may use the title if certified by the State Department of Education (see Chapter 1.6);

---

1. Mass. Gen. L. ch. 112, § 118; 251 CMR 3.04 (1).
2. Mass. Gen. L. ch. 112, § 122.
3. Mass. Gen. L. ch. 112, § 123.

3. students of psychology who are pursuing an official course of graduate study at an approved educational institution may use the title in conjunction with activities and services that are a part of a supervised training program if the word *psychological trainee* or *psychological intern* appears; and

4. persons eligible for licensure who provide services for no more than 1 day per month may use the title.

Individuals who are not registered with the Board or who do not meet one of the exceptions may not call themselves psychologists. They may independently practice, however, if they use some other title (e.g., psychotherapist) that is not regulated by law in Massachusetts. Other than the exceptions described above, Massachusetts does not recognize subdoctoral psychologists. This has important implications for third-party reimbursement that apply only to licensed psychologists. (See Chapter 3.1.)

Rights and Responsibilities of Subdoctoral and Unlicensed Psychologists

Even if a person can use the title psychologist because of an exemption from licensure, he or she may not have all the legal benefits of a licensed psychologist. For example, confidentiality and privileged communications laws (see Chapters 4.2 and 4.3) do not apply.[4] Unlicensed psychologists are ineligible for insurance reimbursement. (See Chapter 3.1.) With regard to malpractice (see Chapter 6.5), it is unclear whether a subdoctoral or exempted psychologist would be held to the same standard of care as a licensed psychologist or to the standard of an unlicensed psychologist of the same class.

Alternative Licensure

A master's-level psychologist with a subspecialization in counseling may be licensed as a mental health counselor by the Board of Allied Mental Health and Human Services Professions.[5]

---

4. Commonwealth v. Mandeville, 386 Mass. 393, 436 N.E.2d 912 (1982).
5. Mass. Gen. L. ch. 112, § 165, as amended by St. 1990, ch. 477, § 5.

1.5

Licensure and Regulation of Social Workers

The licensure and regulation of social workers is governed by statutes that establish a Board of Registration of Social Workers, define terms contained within the law, set qualifications and procedures for licensure of social workers, regulate the conduct of licensed social workers, provide for administrative hearings and a social worker–client privilege, and prescribe criminal sanctions for violations of the chapter.[1]

Board of Registration of Social Workers

The Board of Registration of Social Workers (Board) is the primary administrative body that licenses and regulates social workers. It consists of seven members appointed by the governor for 3-year terms. Four members must be social workers from each of the types of social workers eligible for licensure. The Board has the duty to:[2]

1. regulate the granting, denial, revocation, renewal, probation, and suspension of licenses;

2. prescribe the fees, forms, and timetables for the certification process;

3. keep records and establish rules of confidentiality for dissemination of the records;

---

1. Mass. Gen. L. ch. 13, § 80; Mass. Gen. L. ch. 112, §§ 130–137; 258 CMR 1.00 *et seq.*
2. Mass. Gen. L. ch. 13, § 80.

4. investigate charges of violations of the statutes;

5. prescribe continuing education requirements; and

6. establish a mechanism for receipt of consumer complaints.[3]

Licensure

The law[4] describes four categories of social workers eligible for licensure.

Licensed Social Worker

A licensed social worker must possess a doctorate or master's degree in social work, pass an examination prepared by the Board or the equivalent national examination, and not be in violation of standards for professional conduct.

Social Worker

A social worker must possess a baccalaureate degree in social work or in another field and 2 years of full-time work experience or the equivalent. In addition, a person with at least 5 years of work experience may, with the Board's approval, substitute up to 4 years of work experience for 2 years of education. The individual must also pass the state or national examination and not be in violation of standards for professional conduct.

Social Work Associate

A social work associate must possess a baccalaureate or an associate in arts degree in a human services field or substitute the equivalent of 2 years of full-time work experience in a social service setting for each year of the educational requirement. The candidate must also pass the appropriate state or national examination and not be in violation of standards for professional conduct.

Independent Clinical Social Worker

An independent clinical social worker must possess the qualifications for licensure as a social worker; have the equivalent of 3 years of work experience in the field of clinical social work, 2 of which are subsequent to receipt of a master's degree; and pass the appropriate state or national examination.

---

3. Mass. Gen. L. ch. 13, § 84.
4. Mass. Gen. L. ch. 112, § 131; see 258 CMR 12.00.

Advantages of Licensure

The statute protecting the confidentiality of communications between a social worker and a client[5] only applies to social workers who are licensed.[6] (See Chapter 4.2.)

Exceptions to the Regulations

The law does not restrict the activities and services of all persons who may engage in social work.

First, employees of government agencies may be licensed as social workers if they are employed for 6 months and have passed the equivalent civil service examination.[7] In addition, physicians, nurses, attorneys, psychologists, marriage and family counselors (see Chapter 1.8), school psychologists and counselors, occupational therapists, members of the clergy, and rehabilitation counselors may incidentally practice social work if they do not hold themselves out to be social workers.[8]

Second, students of social work may practice social work if they are clearly identified as a *social work trainee* or *social work intern*.[9] Finally, employees of government agencies may call themselves *social workers* if they are employed as such by government agencies.[10]

Regulation

The law concerning regulation specifies reasons for suspension or revocation of licenses, the powers of the Board to remedy violations, violation classifications, appeal procedures, and confidentiality (see Chapter 4.2) and privileged communications (see Chapter 4.3) requirements.

Violations

A social worker's license may be suspended, revoked, or placed on probationary status for:[11]

---

5. Mass. Gen. L. ch. 112, § 135A.
6. Commonwealth v. Collett, 387 Mass. 424, 439 N.E.2d 1223 (1982).
7. Mass. Gen. L. ch. 112, § 131.
8. Mass. Gen. L. ch. 112, § 134.
9. *Id.*
10. *Id.*
11. Mass. Gen. L. ch. 112, § 137.

1. conviction of a felony involving moral turpitude in the practice of social work, or

2. fraud or deceit in connection with obtaining a license.

As with the other boards of registration, the Board of Registration of Social Workers has procedures for reviewing, investigating, and processing complaints. Complaints that survive initial inquiry may become the subject of full disciplinary proceedings.[12] After a hearing, the Board may restrict or terminate a license.[13]

---

12. 258 CMR 1.00 *et seq.*
13. 258 CMR 30.00 *et seq.*

1.6

Licensure, Certification, and Regulation of School and Educational Psychologists

The Massachusetts Department of Education (Department) certifies persons in school psychology if they are employed in primary and secondary school settings.[1] The certification is entirely independent of the Board of Registration of Psychologists. School psychologists are exempted from licensure by the Board of Registration of Psychologists. School psychologists may be licensed by the Board of Registration of Allied Mental Health and Human Services Professions.[2]

Certification

The rules governing school psychology certification require:[3] 60 graduate semester hours in psychology and 600 clock hours of practicum, at least two-thirds of which must be in a school.

A school psychologist is supposed to know psychological principles and theories, diagnostic techniques, and consultation methods.[4]

Licensure of Educational Psychologists

Persons certified as school psychologists who have a Master's degree and 2 years of supervised training and who pass a licensure

---

1. Mass. Gen. L. ch. 112, § 123(b); Mass. Gen. L. ch. 112, §§ 130–137.
2. Mass. Gen. L. ch. 112, § 163.
3. 603 CMR 7.04 (54).
4. 603 CMR 7.04 (54) (b) (c) (d) (e).

examination can be licensed as educational psychologists by the Board of Registration of Allied Mental Health and Human Services Professions.[5] This license applies to activities in a school setting but does not authorize the psychologist to practice privately.[6]

---

5. Mass. Gen. L. ch. 112, § 165, as amended by St. 1990, ch. 477.
6. Mass. Gen. L. ch. 112, § 163, as amended by St. 1989, ch. 720.

1.7

Endorsement and Regulation of School Counselors

The State Board of Education (Board) certifies guidance counselors employed in primary and secondary school settings. The certification is not required for activities outside of the school setting.[1]

Requirements

The Board sets out two requirements for guidance counselor certification:[2]

1. a Massachusetts teaching certificate and successful completion of a 150-hour practicum, or
2. 30 semester hours of graduate study and completion of a 300-hour practicum.

A guidance counselor is expected to (a) know psychology and developmental theory, (b) understand and be able to communicate with persons of varied backgrounds and abilities, (c) help students be responsible for their behavior, (d) work with appropriate agencies in effectively counseling students.[3]

---

1. 603 CMR 7.04 (53).
2. 603 CMR 7.04 (53).
3. 603 CMR 7.04 (53) (b) (c) (d) (e) (f).

1.8

Licensure and Regulation of Marriage and Family Therapists

In Massachusetts, the Board of Registration of Allied Health and Human Services Professionals (Board) licenses marriage and family therapists.[1] The Board consists of 11 persons appointed by the governor.[2] Of the members of the Board, two must be marriage and family therapists.[3] Licensure requires a master's degree in a related field, two years of supervised experience, and passage of an examination.[4] A person using the term *licensed marriage and family therapist* without being licensed by the Board is guilty of a crime that carries a $500 fine.[5] As with other licensing boards, the Board has authority to investigate allegations of unprofessional conduct and impose discipline as appropriate.[6] Discipline may result from unprofessional conduct or from conviction of a crime that in the opinion of the Board renders the person unfit to practice. Before taking disciplinary action, the Board must conduct a hearing in which the accused person must be presented with the evidence against him or her and be given an opportunity to rebut it.[7]

---

1. Mass. Gen. L. ch. 112, § 165.
2. Mass. Gen. L. ch. 13, § 88.
3. Mass. Gen. L. ch. 13, § 89.
4. Mass. Gen. L. ch. 112, § 165.
5. Mass. Gen. L. ch. 112, § 171.
6. Mass. Gen. L. ch. 112, § 169.
7. *Id.*

1.9

Certification and Regulation of Hypnotists

In some states, the law regulates hypnosis and the professional title *hypnotist* by prescribing education, experience, and skills. In these states MHPs would have to obtain certification to use the title of hypnotist. Since Massachusetts does not have such a law, MHPs may use the title hypnotist at their own discretion. There is law governing the use of hypnotically induced testimony in the courtroom. (See Chapter 5D.12.) Massachusetts law does make it clear that laws pertaining to registration of physicians do not apply to "clairvoyants or persons practicing hypnotism. . . ."[1] This suggests that although the Commonwealth recognizes that hypnotists exist, it has not chosen to specially license them.

---

1. Mass. Gen. L. ch. 112, § 7.

1.10

Licensure and Regulation of Polygraph Examiners

Massachusetts licenses polygraph examiners through its licensing procedure for private investigators. A person must receive a license from the Commissioner of Public Safety to serve as a private investigator or private detective.[1] The individual must be 25 years of age and have had 3 years of detective or investigative work experience with a police department or similar public agency.[2] The statutory definition of *private detective* or *private investigator* includes persons who use lie detectors.[3]

---

1. Mass. Gen. L. ch. 147, § 23.
2. Mass. Gen. L. ch. 147, § 25.
3. Mass. Gen. L. ch. 147, § 22.

1.11

Open Meeting Laws

Massachusetts has a strong open meeting law that makes available to the public the deliberations and records of public agencies.[1] The open meeting law requirements apply to "governmental bodies." These bodies include every state or county agency, board, and commission and every region, district, city, or town committee and subcommittee. They also include the governing boards of local housing, redevelopment, transportation, and other similar authorities.[2] Before an agency, including a credentialing authority, can hold a meeting, notice must be posted in a public location 48 hours in advance.[3]

Certain matters that governmental bodies consider require privacy. The law allows these matters to be handled behind closed doors, with the public excluded.[4] These private sessions are known as executive sessions and are part of public meetings. After a regular public meeting is convened, the governmental body may announce (usually after conducting public business) that it is going into executive session for a stated purpose. The presiding officer must state the purpose and whether the open meeting will reconvene after the executive session.[5] A majority of the members must vote to go into executive session, and the vote of each member must be recorded as a roll call vote and entered into the minutes.[6]

---

1. Mass. Gen. L. ch. 30A, §§ 11A and 11A-1/2; Mass. Gen. L. ch. 34, § 9G; Mass. Gen. L. ch. 39, § 23B.
2. Mass. Gen. L. ch. 30A, §§ 11A and 11A-1/2 (state bodies).
3. Mass. Gen. L. ch. 30A, § 11A-1/2; Mass. Gen. L. ch. 34, § 9G; Mass. Gen. L. ch. 39, § 23B.
4. *Id.*
5. Mass. Gen. L. ch. 30A, § 11A-1/2.
6. District Attorney v. Board of Selectmen of Sunderland, 11 Mass. App. Ct. 663, 418 N.E.2d 642 (1981).

There are several grounds for holding executive sessions. Executive sessions may be held to discuss the reputation, character, physical condition, or mental health of an individual.[7] Because individual privacy is the justification for excluding the public, the individual being discussed has the right to have the hearing in public. If an executive session is held, the individual concerned (and his or her attorney or representative) has the right to be present. The individual is entitled to 48 hours advance written notification of the proposed executive session, unless waived by agreement of the parties.

Executive sessions may also be held to consider complaints against public employees, to discuss strategy for collective bargaining, to investigate criminal complaints, and for other similar reasons.

A governmental body must make a record of each meeting. Generally, such records are public information. Records of executive sessions may be kept closed if making them available to the public would defeat the lawful purpose of the executive session.[8]

The open meeting law is enforced by the attorney general or the district attorney or by a private lawsuit.[9]

---

7. Mass. Gen. L. ch. 30A, § 11A-1/2.
8. *Id.*
9. See Gerstein v. Superintendent Search Screening Committee, 405 Mass. 465, 541 N.E.2d 984 (1989).

Section 2

Forms of
Business
Practice

2.1

Sole Proprietorships

Mental health professionals who practice alone and without any formal organization are termed *sole proprietors*. Unlike partnerships and professional corporations (see Chapters 2.2 and 2.3), there is no state law directly regulating this type of business entity. Sole practitioners should be aware of federal and state tax laws affecting their practice.

2.2

Professional Corporations

Mental health professionals who do not work for an employer as a salaried employee typically organize their business in one of three forms: sole proprietorship (see Chapter 2.1), partnership (see Chapter 2.3), or professional corporation (PC).

Benefits of Incorporation

There are two main benefits to MHPs incorporating their practices. First, certain tax deductions are available only to a PC (e.g., for the purchase of health insurance, death benefits, and retirement plans). Second, incorporation may limit liability for the shareholders.

Incorporation and Operation Procedures

A PC may be organized for the purpose of engaging in more than one category of professional service.[1] For example, a psychologist and a social worker may organize a professional corporation. The organizers are the owners or stockholders of the corporation.[2] The corporate name must contain the words *professional corporation, corporation, incorporated,* or the abbreviation for one of these.[3] The corporate name need not reflect the names of the incorporators.

---

1. Mass. Gen. L. ch. 156A, § 3(b); *see* 950 CMR 105.03.
2. Mass. Gen. L. ch. 156A, § 10.
3. Mass. Gen. L. ch. 156A, § 8.

Liability and Accountability

Each shareholder of a corporation is liable only to the extent of his or her shareholdings; liability is no greater than that of a shareholder of a regular business corporation.[4]

Operation of the Professional Corporation

A professional corporation is created by filing articles of organization with the Massachusetts Secretary of State and by adopting by-laws.[5] The corporation is managed by its officers and directors. The directors are elected by the shareholders, the officers by the directors. The officers must be professionals eligible to create a professional corporation. Elections must be held each year at an annual meeting. Shareholders may sell shares, vote to merge the corporation or to dissolve it, and make other decisions necessary to the operation of the business.[6]

Annual reports must be filed with the secretary of state.[7] The annual report lists the officers and directors of the corporation.

---

4. Mass. Gen. L. ch. 156A, § 6.
5. 950 CMR 105.00 *et seq.*
6. Mass. Gen. L. ch. 156A, §§ 10–16.
7. Mass. Gen. L. ch. 156A, § 18.

2.3

Partnerships

A partnership is an association of two or more persons to carry on a for-profit business.[1] The partnership is a legal entity in whose name the business is conducted.

Formation of a Partnership

A partnership is formed when two or more persons agree to be co-owners of a business for profit.[2] The intent to share profits is the most important factor in determining whether a partnership exists. For example, two psychiatrists who share office space will not be a partnership unless they also intend to share the profits of their services.

Partners do not have to share equally in profits and losses. Generally, profits are assigned to the partners according to their respective shares in the partnership. For example, where a partnership consists of two persons, one of whom initially contributed $50,000 and the other $100,000, the latter may legitimately claim two-thirds of the profits. The partners may agree, however, to allocate partnership income and losses in different proportions. Partners should set out the relative risks and benefits they intend to share in a partnership agreement.

---

1. Mass. Gen. L. ch. 108A, § 6(1).
2. Mass. Gen. L. ch. 108A, § 6.

Rights and Duties Between Partners

Partners have equal rights in the management and conduct of business.[3] Each partner has the right to inspect the partnership books,[4] to receive all information that may affect the partnership,[5] to demand a formal accounting,[6] and to rely on the other partners to report all benefits to the partnership.[7]

The law views each partner as an agent of the partnership: Each person's acts binds the other partners as long as the acts are within the partner's authority.[8] In no event can a partner individually assign the partnership property in trust to creditors, dispose of the goodwill of the business, make it impossible to carry on the ordinary business of the partnership, acknowledge responsibility in any lawsuit against the partnership, or submit a partnership claim or liability to arbitration.[9]

Perhaps most important, any wrongful act or omission of any partner acting in the ordinary course of the business of the partnership that results in a loss, injury, or penalty accrues to all of the partners.[10] Therefore, if any partner misapplies money or property of a third party, the partnership is responsible.[11] The partners are jointly and severally liable for wrongful acts, which means that a wronged person may sue one, several, or all of the partners.[12]

Dissolution of a Partnership

A partnership is dissolved by:[13]

1. the terms of the partnership agreement;
2. the express will of any partner to dissolve the partnership when no definite term or particular undertaking is specified in the agreement;
3. the expulsion of any partner from the business in accordance with such a power conferred by the partnership agreement;

---

3. Mass. Gen. L. ch. 108A, § 9.
4. *Id.*
5. *Id.*
6. *Id.*
7. *Id.*
8. *Id.*
9. *Id.*
10. Mass. Gen. L. ch. 108A, § 11.
11. Mass. Gen. L. ch. 108A, § 14.
12. Mass. Gen. L. ch. 108A, § 15.
13. Mass. Gen. L. ch. 108A, § 31.

4. a violation of the agreement where one of the partners expressly intends to dissolve the partnership;

5. any event that makes it unlawful for the business of the partnership to be carried on or for the members to carry it on;

6. the death of any partner;

7. the bankruptcy of any partner or the partnership; or

8. the decree of a court when:

   a. a partner has been declared in any judicial proceeding to be incompetent,[14]

   b. a partner becomes in any other way incapable of performing his or her part of the partnership contract,

   c. a partner is guilty of conduct that tends to prejudice the conduct of the business,

   d. a partner willfully or persistently breaches the partnership agreement or otherwise conducts him- or herself in matters relating to the partnership so that it is not practicable to carry on the business in partnership with that partner,

   e. the business of the partnership can only be carried on at a loss, or

   f. other circumstances render a dissolution equitable.

Generally, the dissolution of a partnership terminates the authority of the partners except to conclude the partnership's affairs.[15] This does not, however, absolve the partners of whatever liability may have accrued to the partnership before dissolution. After dissolution, some of the partners may form a new partnership. Although it may operate under the same name as the earlier entity, it would legally be a new entity.

---

14. Mass. Gen. L. ch. 108A, § 32.
15. Mass. Gen. L. ch. 108A, § 33.

2.4

Health Maintenance Organizations

A health maintenance organization (HMO) is a health care provider that an individual or a group pays a single fee to and receives health care services at little or no additional cost.[1] HMOs are regulated by the commissioner of insurance.[2] Employees of the HMO or professionals who contract with the organization on a fee-for-service basis provide the health care services.

Benefits for Mental Health Services

The law[3] provides that an HMO must offer basic health care services. Some HMOs are *closed panel* systems offering subscribers a choice among employee physicians; others are *open panel* permitting subscribers to choose their own physician. (See also Chapter 2.6.) HMOs have grown rapidly in recent years. Many employ MHPs and offer mental health coverage.

---

1. Mass. Gen. L. ch. 176G, § 14.
2. *Id.*
3. *Id.*

2.5

Preferred Provider Organizations

A Preferred Provider Organization (PPO) is an organization of health care providers that offers health care services to a given group for a fee in return for an exclusive service arrangement with that group. The service providers see the patients in the providers' own offices.

In Massachusetts, PPOs have generally been established by insurance companies that have then marketed their PPO program to physicians and hospitals to provide service for a fee to groups that are given a limited choice of provider options. The theory behind PPOs is that in exchange for a guaranteed market, providers will give consumers a discount in price.

In Massachusetts, PPOs are regulated as HMOs. This means that a prospective PPO must file required documents with the commissioner of insurance,[1] and the commissioner has the authority to disapprove rates charged to patients if he or she finds the rates excessive, inadequate, or unfairly discriminatory.[2]

1. Mass. Gen. L. ch. 176G, § 14.
2. Mass. Gen. L. ch. 176G, § 16.

2.6

Individual Practice Associations

An Individual Practice Association (IPA) is a form of HMO; it acts as a decentralized HMO. An IPA does not have a central site for providing health care service but contracts with employers to provide services. The members of the IPA practice in their own offices or in small groups, and they are compensated by the organization on a fee-for-service or fee-per-patient basis. Unlike a PPO, IPAs have exclusive service contracts.

As discussed in Chapter 2.4, IPAs, like HMOs, are regulated by Massachusetts law. They must register with the commissioner of insurance,[1] and the commissioner has the authority to disapprove rates charged by the IPA as being excessive, inadequate, or unfairly discriminatory.[2]

1. Mass. Gen. L. ch. 176G, § 14.
2. Mass. Gen. L. ch. 176G, § 16.

Hospital, Administrative, and Staff Privileges

The law in certain states governs which classes of MHPs are eligible for hospital staff privileges, i.e., membership on the hospital's medical staff. Massachusetts has traditionally regulated physician staff privileges at hospitals.[1] Recent legislation has sought to prevent discrimination against psychologists and licensed independent clinical social workers in granting hospital staff privileges.[2]

Hospital Staff Privileges

To practice in a hospital, including the right to admit patients, a physician or MHP must be admitted to privileges.[3] The standards for admission to privileges are set forth in the hospital's by-laws. By-laws must comply with procedures authorized by the Joint Commission on Accreditation of Hospitals (JCAH).[4] Massachusetts law requires hospital by-laws to contain provisions for reporting misconduct by a health care provider to the board that regulates the provider.[5]

In general, to meet legal requirements, by-laws must contain provisions governing the admission of health care providers to

---

1. Mass. Gen. L. ch. 111, § 203.
2. Mass. Gen. L. ch. 19, § 19; Mass. Gen. L. ch. 111, § 51F, as amended by St. 1989 ch. 120.
3. Brant, *Representing the Physician in Staff Privilege Cases in Massachusetts*, 29 BOSTON B. J. 33 (Mar.–Apr. 1985).
4. Adjunct Task Force, Massachusetts Hospital Association, AN ANALYSIS OF THE REVISED MEDICAL STAFF STANDARDS (1984).
5. Mass. Gen. L. ch. 111, § 203 (a).

privileges[6] and a description of procedures to be followed before privileges can be suspended or rescinded.[7] Court review of decisions to suspend or terminate privileges is usually limited to whether the hospital followed its by-laws[1] procedures.[8]

Hospital Peer Committee

Every licensed hospital must have a peer-review committee composed of members of the medical staff to review the professional practices within the hospital to evaluate the quality of care provided by the institution.[9] Any action taken by a hospital peer review committee or a medical society affecting medical staff privileges or society membership must be reported to the Board of Registration in Medicine.[10] The Board of Registration in Medicine cannot obtain records from a peer review committee before formal charges are brought against a physician.[11]

---

6. Bello v. South Shore Hospital, 384 Mass. 770, 429 N.E.2d 1011 (1981).
7. Duby v. Baron, 369 Mass. 614, 341 N.E.2d 870 (1976).
8. Duby v. Jordan Hospital, 369 Mass. 626, 341 N.E.2d 876 (1976).
9. Mass. Gen. L. ch. 111, § 1 and 53B.
10. Mass. Gen. L. ch. 111, § 53B and § 203.
11. Commonwealth v. Choate-Symmes Health Services, Inc., 406 Mass. 27, 545 N.E.2d 1167 (1989).

2.8

Zoning for Community Homes

Local communities have the authority to zone parts of the community for residential or commercial activities. A Massachusetts statute limits the power of cities and towns to regulate residential placements for mentally ill or mentally retarded persons or for ex-offenders. These community homes are exempt from local zoning.[1] This is due to a provision in the state zoning code that exempts from local zoning any use for an *educational purpose*.[2] The Massachusetts courts have consistently held that community residences meet the statutory requirement of being for educational purposes, and thus, local zoning cannot be used to exclude such homes.[3] Attempts at local regulation or exclusion have repeatedly failed. Nonetheless, organizations seeking to create community programs are well advised to work with area residents to lessen potential community hostility.[4]

1. Tuoni, *Deinstitutionalization and Community Resistance by Zoning Restrictions*, 66 MASS. L. REV. 125 (1981).
2. Mass. Gen. L. ch. 40A, § 3.
3. Fitchburg Housing Authority v. Board of Zoning Appeals of Fitchburg, 380 Mass. 869, 406 N.E.2d 1006 (1980).
4. Tuoni, at 138.

Insurance Reimbursement and Deductions for Services

3.1

Insurance Reimbursement for Services

Health insurance policies in Massachusetts must provide reimbursement for mental health services, both inpatient and outpatient. This includes services by all licensed MHPs (see Chapter 3.2).[1] Outpatient services must be covered up to $500 in a calendar year.

The statute requiring insurance coverage for mental health services applies to all health coverage including that provided by HMOs. MHPs covered include psychiatrists, psychologists, licensed independent clinical social workers, and psychiatric nurses.[2]

---

1. Mass. Gen. L. ch. 175, § 47B. *See* Metropolitan Life Insurance Co. v. Massachusetts, 471 U.S. 724, 105 S. Ct. 2380 (1985).
2. *Id.*

Mental Health Benefits in State Insurance Plans

As noted in Chapter 3.1, all health insurance plans in Massachusetts must include specific mental health benefits.[1] The coverage applies to any "mental or nervous condition," as described in the standard nomenclature of the American Psychiatric Association.[2]

Each health insurance policy, whether individual or group, must provide coverage for at least 60 days of inpatient care at a public or private mental health facility and coverage equal to that for any other illness at an accredited general hospital.[3] A unique aspect of the Massachusetts law is its requirement for $500 of outpatient coverage.[4] The insurance industry challenged the law mandating health insurance coverage for mental health services, but a unanimous decision of the United States Supreme Court upheld the validity of the law.[5]

---

1. Mass. Gen. L. ch. 175, § 47B.
2. *Id.*
3. Mass. Gen. L. ch. 175, § 47B(b).
4. Mass. Gen. L. ch. 175, § 47B(c).
5. Metropolitan Life Insurance Co. v. Massachusetts, 471 U.S. 724, 105 S. Ct. 2380 (1985).

3.3

Tax Deductions for Services

Payments for mental health services may be deductible as either an individual medical deduction or as a business expense. Whether or not a deduction is allowed depends on the nature of the service and the use by the recipient–taxpayer.[1]

Mental Health Services as a Medical Deduction

Professional services relating to the diagnosis or treatment of mental or emotional disorders are allowable as medical deductions under both federal and state law. Federal law allows for a deduction for services performed by psychiatrists and psychologists who are qualified and authorized under state law.[2]

The Internal Revenue Service (IRS) also allows deductions for payments made to other types of providers.[3] Accordingly, payments for medical services rendered by practitioners such as chiropractors, social workers, or psychotherapists constitute medical expenses and are deductible for federal income tax purposes to the extent provided by law.[4] Federal law does not require that the practitioners who perform the services be licensed or officially certified in order for the expenses to be deductible.

---

1. IRS Rev. Rul. 143, 1953-2 C.B. 129.
2. IRS Rev. Rul. 91, 1963-1 C.B. 1.
3. *Id.*
4. *Id.*

Mental Health Services as a Business Deduction

Expenses for mental health services provided to employees are deductible to businesses as trade or business expenses. Therefore, if a business provides an employee assistance program, it may deduct the cost of the program on its corporate income tax form as an ordinary business expense.[5] Massachusetts allows limited deductions for medical care from the state income tax.

---

5. Welch v. Helvering, 290 U.S. 111 (1933).

Privacy of Professional Information

4.1

Extensiveness, Ownership, Maintenance, and Access to Records

Most MHPs maintain records about their clients. Although there is a statutory requirement[1] that hospitals keep records about their patients and the statute permits patient access, there is no legal requirement that MHPs maintain such records in a private setting. If psychiatrists develop records about patients, a new statute requires patient access on request.[2] Patients in Department of Mental Health facilities do not have automatic access to their records unless the superintendent of the facility (officially called the chief operating officer) determines that there is no harm in providing such access.[3] Attorneys for patients will be granted access on request.[4]

Liability for Violation

MHPs own the patient records they maintain. As discussed in Chapter 4.2, most communications between MHPs and clients, whether oral or written, are protected from disclosure by confidentiality statutes. In addition, patients have a common law right to expect confidentiality in their communications with MHPs.[5] The Board of Registration in Medicine has censured physicians for im-

---

1. Mass. Gen. L. ch. 111, § 70.
2. Mass. Gen. L. ch. 112, § 12CC, added by St. 1990, ch. 370.
3. Mass. Gen. L. ch. 123, § 36; *see also* 257 CMR 3.07 (5) (a–e).
4. Doe v. Commissioner of Mental Health, 372 Mass. 534, 362 N.E.2d 920 (1977).
5. Alberts v. Devine, 395 Mass. 59, 479 N.E.2d 113 (1985).

proper disclosure of patient information.[6] In addition to professional sanctions, improper disclosure can subject an MHP to a civil suit for damages for invasion of privacy.[7]

6. Ryan v. Board of Registration in Medicine, 388 Mass. 1013, N.E.2d 1070 (1983).
7. Tower v. Hirschhorn, 397 Mass. 581, 492 N.E.2d 728 (1986).

4.2

Confidential Relations and Communications

Generally, a confidential communication is either written or verbal information conveyed by the client to an MHP in the course of a professional relationship. Confidentiality originated in professional ethics codes[1] from a belief that effective psychotherapy required a guarantee from the therapist that no information obtained in the course of evaluation or treatment would be given to others. In Massachusetts, social workers[2] are held to a standard similar to that of psychologists and psychiatrists. Requirements of confidentiality exist in addition to privilege statutes (see Chapter 4.3) that limit court testimony. These requirements are rooted in the common law. MHPs may be sued for improper release of confidential information.[3]

Psychologists

Psychologists Covered Under These Statutes

All communications between licensed psychologists and their clients are confidential. However, the extent of confidentiality has limits that must be revealed to clients at the initiation of services.[4] The limitations on confidentiality include situations where the client presents a clear and present danger to him- or herself and refuses

---

1. American Psychological Association, *Ethical Principles of Psychologists*, 36 AM. PSYCHOL. 633–638 (1981).
2. Mass. Gen. L. ch. 112, § 135A and 135B; *see also* Commonwealth v. Collett, 387 Mass. 424, 439 N.E.2d 1223 (1982).
3. Allen v. Holyoke Hospital, 398 Mass. 372, 496 N.E.2d 1368 (1986).
4. Mass. Gen. L. ch. 112, § 129A.

to accept further appropriate treatment.[5] There is also an exception for situations where the patient discloses the intention to commit a crime.[6] A psychologist is authorized to take steps to protect a third person whom a client threatens during a therapy session.[7] Those steps include notifying the individual, notifying appropriate law-enforcement persons, or arranging to have the patient hospitalized voluntarily or involuntarily.

Limitations on The Duty

The duty regarding confidentiality has many limitations. First, if a psychologist learns while rendering services that the client intends to inflict serious bodily harm on another person, the psychologist must take reasonable steps to warn the intended victim or law enforcement officials.[8] Further, psychologists have a duty to report nonaccidental injuries and neglect of minors (see Chapter 5A.8) and adults (see Chapter 5A.7) to proper authorities.[9] Third, a psychologist may disclose the fact of having treated a client in order to collect fees owed for the services rendered.[10]

Liability for Violation

Several types of penalties may be imposed for violations of confidentiality. The Board of Registration of Psychologists may suspend or revoke the license of a psychologist for breach of ethical standards including confidentiality.[11] The decision to revoke or suspend is enforceable by a petition in equity to ensure enforcement pending final determination.[12]

Clients harmed by a breach of confidentiality may also bring a civil suit for recovery of damages based on several legal theories (see Chapter 6.5).

Psychiatrists

Scope of the Duty

The only statutory limitation on psychiatrists revealing information is in the privilege statute (see Chapter 4.3). However, there is a common law duty on psychiatrists not to reveal the contents of

---

5. *Id.*
6. *Id.*
7. *Id.*
8. *Id.*
9. Mass. Gen. L. ch. 119, § 51A.
10. 251 CMR 3.04.
11. *Id.*
12. Mass. Gen. L. ch. 112, § 128.

therapy communications without consent of the client.[13] Psychiatrists do have a duty to protect third parties from harm if they become aware of a threat to a third party by alerting the threatened person or law enforcement authorities or by taking steps to hospitalize the client.[14]

Social Workers

Scope of Duty

Social workers are under a statutory duty not to reveal confidential communications with clients in most circumstances.[15] A social worker may disclose information (a) by written consent of the person or one otherwise authorized to do so, (b) where the communication "reveals the contemplation or commission of a crime or harmful act," or (c) where the client brings "charges" against the social worker.[16] As with psychiatrists and psychologists, confidentiality may be breached by requirements to report child (see Chapter 5A.8) or adult abuse (see Chapter 5A.7). As with psychologists, social workers must reveal the limits of confidentiality during the initial phase of a professional relationship. In the face of a threat against another person, the social worker must inform that person, inform an appropriate law enforcement person, or arrange for voluntary or involuntary hospitalization of the client.[17]

Marriage and Family Counselors, Educational Psychologists, Rehabilitation Counselors, and Mental Health Counselors

Persons licensed as marriage and family counselors, educational psychologists, rehabilitation counselors, and mental health counselors by the Board of Registration of Allied Mental Health and Human Services Professionals are required to maintain confidentiality of communications with clients unless the client consents to

---

13. Tower v. Hirschhorn, 397 Mass. 581, 492 N.E.2d 728 (1986).
14. Mass. Gen. L. ch. 233, § 20B, as amended by St. 1989, ch. 117; Mass. Gen. L. ch. 123, § 36B.
15. Mass. Gen. L. ch. 112, § 135A.
16. Mass. Gen. L. ch. 112, § 135B.
17. Mass. Gen. L. ch. 112, § 135A.

a release, reveals the contemplation or commission of a crime, sues the counselor, or is involved in a criminal proceeding and revelation of information is necessary to protect the rights of a defendant.[18]

---

18. Mass. Gen. L. ch. 112, § 172.

4.3

Privileged
Communications

Privilege statutes are exceptions to the general principle of law that all persons must testify to what they know about an event.[1] The concept of privilege is that an effective therapy relationship requires a guarantee from the therapist that no information obtained in the course of evaluation or treatment would be given to others, including courts. Massachusetts has several privilege statutes. They apply only to the issue of court testimony by an MHP. The courts construe privileges narrowly.[2] (See also Chapter 4.2 for confidentiality.)

Psychologists

Psychologists Covered Under These Statutes

The privilege applies only to the communications of licensed psychologists. The law gives a client of a psychologist the privilege of having the psychologist refuse to disclose in a court of law any communication between the client and the psychologist relative to the diagnosis or treatment of the patient's mental or emotional condition.[3]

There are a number of exceptions in which a judge may order that the testimony be given. Generally, the exceptions pertain to child-custody matters and court-related matters such as evaluations

---

1. Commonwealth v. Collett, 387 Mass. 424, 439 N.E.2d 1223 (1982).
2. Commonwealth v. Two Juveniles, 397 Mass. 261, 491 N.E.2d 234 (1986).
3. Mass. Gen. L. ch. 233, § 20B.

for competency to stand trial. There is also an exception where the client brings charges against the psychologist.[4]

A new statute restates the privilege and also serves as a general requirement for confidentiality of communications between psychologists and clients (see Chapter 4.2).[5] This statute does have an exception for situations where the patient discloses the intention to commit a crime.[6] In addition, a recent amendment to the privilege statute makes it clear that the privilege applies to marital and family therapy.[7]

Exceptions to Privilege

Privilege statutes tend to have many exceptions. Indeed, most situations involving court testimony fall within the exceptions rather than the privilege. For example, an exception applies to defendants who raise any mental disability defense in a criminal trial.[8] The defendant is deemed to have waived the psychologist–client privilege as it relates to the defendant's mental state at the time of the alleged crime. (See Chapter 5D.9.) Similarly, an exception applies whenever a psychologist is appointed by the court to examine a criminal defendant to determine whether the defendant is competent to stand trial (see Chapter 5D.5).[9] In this situation, the psychologist must disclose all information concerning the defendant with one exception. The psychologist cannot disclose any statements by the defendant regarding the offense itself unless the defendant consents to the disclosure. A psychologist is protected from being sued by a patient while conducting a court-ordered evaluation.[10] Finally, judges can decide that prospective testimony in child custody cases is more important than maintaining the confidential relationship. Privileges are waived by consent of the client or when the client brings charges against the MHP.[11]

Psychiatrists

Scope of the Duty

Psychiatrists are bound by a privilege statute from giving testimony in court concerning communications with a client unless an exception applies or the client gives consent.[12] The exceptions for psychiatrists are the same as for psychologists (see above).

---

4. *Id.*
5. Mass. Gen. L. ch. 112, § 129A.
6. Mass. Gen. L. ch. 233, § 20B, as amended by St. 1989, ch. 217, § 2.
7. Mass. Gen. L. ch. 233, § 20B, as amended by St. 1989, ch. 270.
8. *Id.*
9. Mass. Gen. L. ch. 123, § 15(b).
10. LaLonde v. Eissner, 405 Mass, 207, 539 N.E.2d 538 (1989).
11. 251 CMR 3.04.
12. Mass. Gen. L. ch. 233, § 20B.

Social Workers

Scope of the Duty

Massachusetts law creates[13] a testimonial privilege between social worker and client that prevents a licensed social worker from testifying about communications with a client unless an exception applies or the client consents. There are many exceptions to the privilege: court-ordered psychiatric examinations; if the client is informed of the possible use of the information in court; when the client brings charges against the social worker; and in custody, adoption, and termination of parental rights cases if a judge determines that the social worker has important evidence and that the best interest of the child is served by allowing the social worker to testify.[14] It should be noted that all other nonconsensual disclosures by a social worker are forbidden without consent, unless the social worker is conducting an abuse or protective service investigation.[15]

Limitations on Privilege

In *Commonwealth v. Collett*,[16] the Massachusetts Supreme Judicial Court ruled that a social worker is not required to treat as confidential communication any information concerning contemplation or commission of a crime or harmful act.

Like the psychotherapist–patient privilege, the social worker–client privilege is available only to persons consulting a *licensed* social worker. The availability of the privilege does not depend on who initiated the relationship or whether the communication came from one who is technically the social worker's client.[17] It is only necessary that the communication came from a person consulting the social worker in his or her professional capacity. Moreover, the privilege does not depend on a person's status in a lawsuit; it protects the confidences of parties and nonparties alike.[18]

In-Camera Hearing

To determine whether otherwise privileged communications should be disclosed because they reveal the contemplation or commission of a crime or harmful act, the trial judge should conduct an in-camera hearing with the social worker. No other parties should be present, and the judge should phrase questions carefully so as to

---

13. Mass. Gen. L. ch. 112, § 135A, as added by St. 1989, ch. 435.
14. *Id.*
15. Commonwealth v. Collett, 387 Mass. 424, 439 N.E.2d 1223 (1982).
16. *Id.*
17. *Id.*
18. *Id.*

limit disclosures to information that falls within the exception. The record of such a hearing should be sealed.[19]

A criminal defendant may have access to the records of a complaining witness held by a psychologist, psychiatrist, or social worker in order to search for bias or motive to lie.[20]

Sexual Assault Counselors

Massachusetts statutes also provide for confidential communications between sexual assault counselors in rape crisis centers. A sexual assault counselor is a person who is employed by, or is a volunteer in, a rape crisis center. This person has undergone 35 hours of training and reports to and is under the direct control and supervision of a licensed social worker, nurse, psychiatrist, psychologist, or psychotherapist. A sexual assault counselor's primary purpose is to render advice, counseling, or assistance to victims of sexual assault.[21]

A rape crisis center is any office, institution, or center offering assistance to victims of sexual assault or to their families. Assistance often includes services such as legal and medical counseling and crisis intervention.[22]

Scope of Duty

The counselor is prohibited from disclosing confidential communications. The statute provides:

> A sexual assault counsellor shall not disclose such confidential communication without prior *written* consent of the victim; provided, however, that nothing in this chapter shall be construed to limit the defendant's right of cross-examination of such counsellor in a civil or criminal proceeding if counsellor testifies with such written consent.[23]

Limitations

All reports, working papers, memoranda, and information received by the counselor are to be confidential without prior written consent of the person who is the subject of the information.[24] Although the statute[25] is written in absolute terms, the Massachusetts Supreme Judicial Court has ruled that where a criminal defendant in

---

19. *Id.*
20. Commonwealth v. Stockhammer, 409 Mass. 867, 570 N.E.2d 992 (1991).
21. Mass. Gen. L. ch. 233, § 20J.
22. *Id.*
23. *Id.*
24. *Id.*
25. *Id.*

a rape trial establishes a need for access to the information held by a sexual assault counselor, a judge may review the material and order it produced.[26]

Domestic Violence Victims' Counselors

A statute provides for confidential communications between a person designated as a domestic violence victims' counselor and victims of domestic violence.[27] A domestic violence counselor is a person who is employed or volunteers in a domestic violence victims' program, who has undergone a minimum of 25 hours of training, who reports to and is under the direct control and supervision of a service supervisor of a domestic violence program, and whose primary purpose is the rendering of advice, counseling, or assistance to victims of abuse.[28] A domestic violence victims' program is any refuge, shelter, office, safe home, institution, or center established for the purpose of offering assistance to victims of abuse through crisis intervention, medical, legal, or support counseling. Any person meeting the statutory requirements as to conditions surrounding employment has a duty to protect any information received in the course of such employment.

Scope of Duty and Limitations

As discussed above, a domestic violence victims' counselor "shall not disclose such confidential communication without prior written consent of victim, except as herein provided."[29] Statutory proscriptions against disclosure of confidential communications are similar to or the same as those for sexual assault counselors.[30]

Confidential Communications to Priests, Rabbis, Ministers, and Christian Science Practitioners

Massachusetts by statute follows the federal Rules of Evidence in extension of privileges concerning confidential communications to recognized religious practitioners. This is an absolute privilege

---

26. Commonwealth v. Two Juveniles, 397 Mass. 261, 491 N.E.2d 234 (1986).
27. Mass. Gen. L. ch. 233, § 20K.
28. Mass. Gen. L. ch. 233, § 20A.
29. Id.
30. Id.

mandating refusal to testify except by consent.[31] It is unclear whether a court would intrude on the relationship between religious leader and congregant to create the same or similar exceptions as have been created in other privileges. Pastoral counselors who come under this privilege should be aware that it is broader than the other statutory privileges. The word *communication* in Massachusetts law[32] is not limited to oral or written conversation and may include other acts by which ideas are transmitted from one person to another.[33]

---

31. Commonwealth v. Zezima, 365 Mass. 238, 310 N.E.2d 590 (1974).
32. Mass. Gen. L. ch. 233, § 20A.
33. Commonwealth v. Zezima, 365 Mass. 238, 310 N.E.2d 590 (1974).

Search, Seizure, and Subpoena of Records

Search of an MHP's office and seizure of any records may occur within the context of a criminal investigation of the MHP or the client.[1] A court may, in certain circumstances, issue a search warrant authorizing the search of an MHP's office. A court may also issue a subpoena requesting that the MHP bring certain records to court.[2]

Search and Seizure

In general, before a government official[3] may search a professional's office, he or she must have a warrant.[4] Although warrantless searches are sometimes permissible, they are generally restricted to exigent circumstances such as immediate danger to a police officer.[5] A search and seizure is typically authorized by a written order from a court clerk directing a police officer to search for specific items. The search warrant will be issued when the magistrate is persuaded that the property or things:[6]

1. to be seized were stolen or embezzled;

2. to be seized were used as a means of committing a criminal offense;

---

1. Commonwealth v. Kobrin, 395 Mass. 284, 479 N.E.2d 674 (1985).
2. *Id.*
3. Thus, this area of law does not govern private individuals acquiring evidence on their own. *See* Commonwealth v. Storella, 6 Mass. App. Ct. 310, 375 N.E.2d 348 (1978).
4. U.S. Const. amend. IV.
5. Commonwealth v. Marchione, 384 Mass. 8, 422 N.E.2d 1362 (1981).
6. Commonwealth v. Markow, 391 Mass. 27, 459 N.E.2d 1225 (1984); *see also* Massachusetts v. Sheppard, 468 U.S. 981 (1984).

3. to be seized are in the possession of a person having the intent to use them as a means of committing a criminal offense, or in possession of another to whom he or she may have delivered it for the purpose of concealing it or preventing it from being discovered;

4. to be seized consist of any item or constitute any evidence that tends to show that a particular criminal offense has been committed or that a particular person has committed a criminal offense; and

5. are to be searched and inspected by an appropriate official in the interest of the public health, safety, and welfare as part of an inspection program authorized by law.[7]

There must be facts tending to establish grounds for the application of the search warrant that are supported by an affidavit naming relevant persons and describing the items and places with specificity.[8] The warrant must be executed within 7 days of being issued.[9] An officer may break into the building if either no response is received within a reasonable time or, after notice of his or her authority and purpose, the officer is refused admittance.[10] Further, the officer may reasonably search any person as a protection against concealed weapons or if it appears that the sought-after property is concealed on the person.[11] Additional property not listed on the warrant but which the officer reasonably believes to be the fruits or instrumentalities of a crime also may be taken.[12]

Although the officer does not have to serve a copy of the warrant before searching,[13] a detailed receipt must be issued for any property taken.[14] Persons objecting to any aspect of a search should contact an attorney since police officers may respond with appropriate force to execute a search warrant. If there is a dispute regarding seized property, a judge will take written testimony from the relevant witnesses to ascertain whether the property is the same as that described in the warrant and if there was probable cause to seize it. If not, the property will be restored to the person from whom it was taken.[15]

---

7. Commonwealth v. Sheppard, 394 Mass. 381, 476 N.E.2d 541 (1985).
8. Commonwealth v. Truax, 397 Mass. 174, 490 N.E.2d 425 (1986).
9. Mass. Gen. L. ch. 276, § 3A.
10. Commonwealth v. Manni, 398 Mass. 741, 500 N.E.2d 807 (1986).
11. Commonwealth v. Madera, 402 Mass. 156, 521 N.E.2d 738 (1988).
12. Commonwealth v. Taylor, 383 Mass. 272, 418 N.E.2d 1226 (1981).
13. Commonwealth v. Upton, 394 Mass. 363, 476 N.E.2d 548 (1985); Arizona v. Hicks, 480 U.S. 321 (1987).
14. Commonwealth v. Varney, 391 Mass. 34, 461 N.E.2d 177 (1984).
15. Id.

Subpoena

A subpoena is a written order of the court compelling a witness to appear and give testimony. It must contain the name of the court, the title of the action, and the time and place where the testimony is to be given.[16] The subpoena may also extend to documentary evidence and other tangible things in the possession or control of the witness.[17] (This is typically referred to as a subpoena duces tecum.) A subpoena is served by delivering a copy directly to the person whose testimony or records are being subpoenaed.[18] Any person who is voluntarily in attendance at a court hearing may be compelled to testify in the same manner as if subpoenaed. Failure to appear at the time and place specified in a subpoena may result in contempt of court proceedings, which can lead to an MHP being jailed.[19]

If producing the subpoenaed documentary evidence would be unreasonable and oppressive, a witness may make a timely motion to quash or modify the subpoena or to condition compliance on payment of the reasonable cost of producing the evidence.[20] Further, it should be noted that mere issuance of a subpoena, which is done by a court clerk, does not indicate that any privilege is overcome. Rather, the MHP must assert the privilege until the client expressly waives it or the court orders the privilege waived as a matter of law, e.g., where the person holding the privilege (the client) disclosed the information in such a way as to extinguish its confidential nature. (See Chapter 4.3). Failure by a psychologist or psychiatrist to initially assert the privilege may result in civil liability (see Chapters 1.1, 1.3, and 6.5) and criminal liability for psychologists (see Chapter 1.3). A hospital must produce a patient's records in response to a subpoena.[21]

---

16. Mass. R. Civ. P. 45(a)
17. Mass. R. Civ. P. 45(b)
18. Mass. R. Civ. P. 45(d)
19. Commonwealth v. Kobrin, 395 Mass. 284, 479 N.E.2d 674 (1985).
20. Mass. R. Civ. P. 45(b).
21. Mass. Gen. L. ch. 111, § 70.

4.5

Access to Public Records

Massachusetts has strong public records laws[1] that enforce a policy of openness and accessibility to governmental records. The basic purpose of public records law is to ensure that governmental activities are open to public examination. There is the presumption of availability of all government records unless exceptions apply.[2]

Definition

There are two major aspects to Massachusetts public records law: one definitional and the other procedural.[3] Records created or held by government agencies can only be kept from the public if they fall within one or more narrow exceptions.[4] Public records are broadly defined to encompass every area of governmental activity. All records are considered public unless specifically exempted by law.[5]

Exemptions/Exceptions

There are 11 statutory exemptions to the public records law. The *first* exemption, exemption (a), applies to records specifically or by

---

1. Mass. Gen. L. ch. 4, § 7, clause 26; Mass. Gen. L. ch. 66, § 10.
2. Brant et al. *Public Records, FIPA and CORI*, 15 SUFFOLK U.L. REV. 23, 24 (1981).
3. W. H. Abrashkin & E. Winsor, FREEDOM OF INFORMATION IN MASSACHUSETTS 4–33 (1989).
4. Mass. Gen. L. ch. 4, § 7, clause 26.
5. *Id.*

necessary implication exempted from disclosure by statute.[6] When a record contains both exempt and nonexempt information, the nonexempt portions are segregated from the exempt portions and can then be disclosed. Since the law presumes that all records are public, the custodian must specify the exemption that applies when denying access.[7] In citing the exemption, the custodian must name the particular statute that exempts the record from disclosure.

Certain statutes specifically exempt records from disclosure. For example, a statute prohibits the disclosure of *impounded birth records* to anyone not legally authorized access.[8] Access is limited to authorized persons only and, therefore, these records are exempted from disclosure under the public records law. Certain other records are also excluded from disclosure.[9]

The *second* exemption, exemption (b),[10] is for records related solely to internal personnel rules and practices of the government unit, provided, however, that such records shall be withheld only to the extent that proper performance of necessary governmental functions requires. This exemption allows the nondisclosure of governmental operating manuals and guidelines relating only to *intra-agency matters* which, if disclosed, would significantly impede the fulfillment of the agency's responsibilities. An instructional manual on computer security would fall under this disclosure exemption.

The *third* exemption, exemption (c),[11] has been the subject of considerable litigation. It exempts personnel and medical files or information, and any other materials or data relating to a specifically named individual, if the disclosure could constitute an unwarranted invasion of personal privacy. The key word in this exemption is *unwarranted*. In applying this exemption, the public's right to know is carefully balanced against the individual's privacy. The record may be withheld only if the extent and seriousness of the invasion of privacy outweighs the public interest. Decisions of the Massachusetts courts have cited welfare payments, alcohol consumption, family fights, and reputation as examples of the information that the privacy exemption is designed to protect.[12] The courts have construed this exemption narrowly to apply only to highly sensitive

---

6. Mass. Gen. L. ch. 4, § 7, clause 26(a).
7. Mass. Gen. L. ch. 66, § 10.
8. Mass. Gen. L. ch. 46, § 2A.
9. Mass. Gen. L. ch. 66, § 17A (Welfare Records); Mass. Gen. L. ch. 62C, § 21(a) (Income Tax Records).
10. Mass. Gen. L. ch. 4, § 7, clause 26(b).
11. Mass. Gen. L. ch. 4, § 7, clause 26(c).
12. Attorney General v. Assistant Commissioner of Real Property Dept., 380 Mass., 623, 404 N.E.2d 1254 (1980); Attorney General v. Collector of Lynn, 377 Mass. 151, 385 N.E.2d 505 (1979); Hastings and Sons Publishing Co. v. Treasurer of Lynn, 374 Mass. 812, 375 N.E.2d 299 (1978).

personal data and the personnel and medical files[13] that are specifically exempted by the language of the statute. A record exempt from disclosure because of the privacy exemption may also be protected by the state privacy act, the Fair Information Practices Act.

The *fourth* exemption, exemption (d),[14] is for inter-agency or intra-agency memoranda or letters relating to policy positions being developed by an agency; however, this exemption does not apply to reasonably completed factual studies or reports on which the development of policy positions was or may have been based. This exemption preserves a degree of confidentiality necessary to the free flow of advice, recommendations, and opinions between persons involved in policy development. By affording protection to individuals whose input may be critical to the quality of the policy ultimately established, this provision encourages candid and complete opinions. Factual materials on which policy positions are being or have been based are not exempt. The exemption applies only to policy positions being developed. Once promulgated, the decision-making process becomes public.[15]

The *fifth* exemption, exemption (e),[16] is for personal notebooks and other materials prepared by an employee of the Commonwealth that are not maintained as part of the files of a governmental unit. In this instance, the exemption protects *written materials that are not made by an individual in his or her capacity as a government employee* and, therefore, are not considered to be a record of the agency. An example would be written information, data, notes, or references to personal matters or activities totally unrelated to the office in which the individual works. This exemption helps protect those records of a personal nature than an employee may keep in his or her desk, file cabinet, or other work station place.

The *sixth* exemption, exemption (f),[17] is for investigatory materials compiled out of the public view by law enforcement or other investigatory officials, the disclosure of which would probably so prejudice effective law enforcement that it would not be in the public interest. This exemption, designed to protect confidential investigative sources, encourages individual citizens to come forward with information and allows law enforcement officials to be candid in recording their investigative observations.

---

13. Globe Newspaper Co. v. Boston Retirement Board, 388 Mass. 427, 446 N.E.2d 1051 (1983).
14. Mass. Gen. L. ch. 4, § 7, clause 26(d).
15. Babets v. Secretary of the Executive Office of Human Services, 403 Mass. 230, 526 N.E.2d 1261 (1988).
16. Mass. Gen. L. ch. 4, § 7, clause 26(e).
17. Mass. Gen. L. ch. 4, § 7, clause 26(f).

The *seventh* exemption, exemption (g),[18] is for trade secrets or commercial or financial information voluntarily provided to an agency for use in developing governmental policy on a promise of confidentiality. This subparagraph, however, does not apply to information submitted as required by law or as a condition of receiving a governmental contract or benefit. For example, a company may provide certain confidential information vital to its interests to the government to assist in public policy making. Such information submitted in confidence may be withheld from disclosure under the public records law. On the other hand, when a company provides data regarding its operations to a government agency in order to secure a contract to do business with the agency, or if such information is required by statute so that the company may be licensed, the records are public.

The *remaining exemptions* all apply to narrow classes of records, including:

(1) proposals and bids to enter into any contract or agreement until the time for the opening of bids in the case of bids to be opened publicly, or until the time for the receipt of bids or proposals has expired in all other cases;

(2) appraisals of real property acquired or to be acquired until a final agreement is entered into, or any litigation relative to such appraisal has been terminated, or the time within which to commence such litigation has expired;[19]

(3) the names and addresses of any persons contained in or referred to in applications for licenses to carry or possess firearms or in firearms identification cards; the names and addresses on sales or transfers of any firearms, rifles, shotguns, machine guns, or ammunition;[20] and the names and addresses on said licenses or cards, and

(4) test questions and answers, scoring keys and sheets, and other examination data used to administer a licensing examination, provided that such materials are used to administer another examination.[21]

Procedures for Obtaining Public Records

The statutory requirements for obtaining public records provide that the person seeking the record should make a written request

---

18. Mass. Gen. L. ch. 4, § 7, clause 26(g).
19. Mass. Gen. L. ch. 4, § 7, clause 26(h).
20. Mass. Gen. L. ch. 4, § 7, clause 26(i).
21. Mass. Gen. L. ch. 4, § 7, clause 26(j).

to the records custodian.[22] Although the records custodian must either provide access to the record or deny the request within a maximum time period of 10 days, the law[23] also states that such access shall be granted without "unreasonable delay." To ensure a prompt response, the request should be made for a specific and identifiable record. The records custodian is obligated only to provide a requester with existing records.

If the records custodian provides access, he or she may charge fees consistent with the statute and applicable regulations of the Supervisor of Public Records.[24] Any portion of a record that is a public record is supposed to be produced.

If a records custodian denies access, he or she must cite the specific exemption that applies.[25] The person requesting the denied record has two choices if he or she wishes to pursue the matter further: (a) seek review by the Supervisor of Public Records, or (b) bring the matter directly to court.[26]

If a person seeks review by the Supervisor of Public Records, the supervisor will review correspondence between the requester and the records custodian and then issue an opinion on whether the records sought are public.[27] If the supervisor rules that the records are public and the records custodian refuses to release them, the supervisor can refer the matter to the attorney general or a district attorney for legal action.[28] Another alternative is that the requester can file suit in superior court directly.[29]

Privacy

In addition to strong public records law, Massachusetts has a state privacy law[30] that protects most government records pertaining to named individuals from disclosure. A government agency is supposed to collect only that amount of personal information that is "reasonably necessary" to do its job.

Agencies are generally not allowed to distribute personal data to any agency or individual other than the data subjects themselves.[31] There are, however, exceptions to this general rule. Personal data may be released to third parties if the data subject con-

---

22. Mass. Gen. L. ch. 66, § 10; 950 CMR 32.00 et seq.
23. Id.
24. Mass. Gen. L. ch. 66, § 10(a); 950 CMR 32.00 et seq.
25. Id.
26. Id.
27. Id.
28. Id.
29. Id.
30. Mass. Gen. L. ch. 66A, § 1 et seq.
31. Mass. Gen. L. ch. 66A, §§ 2(b) and (c).

sents to the disclosure,[32] if disclosure is authorized by a statute or regulation consistent with the law,[33] if there is a medical emergency,[34] or in connection with court proceedings under certain circumstances.[35] On demand, an agency must reveal to a data subject all instances in which personal data on him or her have been released to third parties.[36]

The individual whose records are held is the only person who can police a holder's collection of personal information. A *holder* is a government agency or any private or public entity that contracts with an agency and receives and maintains personal data. If one suspects that a certain agency or other holder is collecting information on him or her, that person can write a letter to the holder asking whether he or she is a data subject.[37] If an individual suspects that a holder is collecting more information than is reasonably necessary, he or she can review relevant records and, if they are overbroad, can ask that the unnecessary data be removed.[38]

Individuals have a right to sue agencies both to correct their records and to collect money damages for violations that have occurred. Successful parties may recover punitive damages and attorney's fees. The attorney general may provide assistance in some cases.[39]

Correcting the Record

Any individual has the right to challenge the accuracy and completeness of the personal information held in his or her file. If a holder has inaccurate information, the first step is to make a written request for correction of the record.[40] This can be done by sending a letter describing the problem to the person in charge of the records and by sending a copy of the letter to the head of the agency that holds the records. If suitable corrections are not made, the individual should then seek a meeting with the person in charge of the records so that they can go over the information together.[41]

If both the record holder and the individual agree that the record is inaccurate, the holder must correct the record. If, however, the holder disagrees with the individual and refuses to change the

---

32. Mass. Gen. L. ch. 66A, § 2(c).
33. Doe v. Registrar of Motor Vehicles, 26 Mass. App. Ct. 415, 528 N.E.2d 880 (1988).
34. Mass. Gen. L. ch. 66A, § 2(c).
35. Mass. Gen. L. ch. 66A, § 2(k); *see* Allen v. Holyoke Hospital, 398 Mass. 372, 496 N.E.2d 1368 (1986).
36. Mass. Gen. L. ch. 66A, § 2(f).
37. Mass. Gen. L. ch. 66A, § 2(b).
38. Mass. Gen. L. ch. 66A, § 2.
39. Mass. Gen. L. ch. 66A, § 2(e).
40. Mass. Gen. L. ch. 66A, § 2(f).
41. Mass. Gen. L. ch. 214, § 3B.

record, the holder must note the individual's claim that the record is not accurate. That note then becomes a part of the individual's personal file. If the holder does not follow these rules for correcting the file, or if the individual is not satisfied with this action and wants to have the file corrected, he or she may seek administrative or judicial review.[42]

Although the correction provisions allow an individual to correct or challenge relevant records, the provisions do not require the holder to send notice of the corrections or challenges to individuals or groups who have already received the information. A person can, however, provide corrections to those who have received his or her personal file.[43]

Administrative Remedies

A holder must permit formal administrative review for any data subject who claims that the holder's personal data on him or her has been handled improperly or is inaccurate.[44] This remedy allows the data subject to correct the record but not to recover money damages for any violations that may have occurred.[45]

If an individual whose rights under the Fair Information Practices Act have been violated is not seeking monetary compensation but wants only to correct the record, the best option is usually administrative review rather than a lawsuit. Results come much faster in an administrative appeal than in a lawsuit, and the cost is much lower.

Each holder must have procedures that enable an individual to challenge improper handling of information and incomplete or inaccurate information in his or her record. Each agency has its own enforcement provisions, but the differences among them are relatively minor. The procedures outlined here are representative of most agencies. If possible, one should check the regulations of the specific agency with which he or she is dealing.[46]

The first step a person seeking administrative review should take is to write a letter of objection to the officer in charge of records or to the head of the agency. The person should describe the violation as specifically as possible and detail the requested remedial action.[47] After the holder receives the letter of objection, he or she has 30 days to notify the agency head, investigate whether the objection is valid, correct the violation if appropriate, and notify the agency head of the action taken. If the holder decides that the

---

42. *Id.*
43. *Id.*
44. 801 CMR 3.04.
45. Mass. Gen. L. ch. 66A, § 2(f).
46. 801 CMR 3.04; 940 CMR 11.03 *et seq.*; 101 CMR 8.01 *et seq.*; 104 CMR 24.10.
47. Mass. Gen. L. ch. 66A, § 2(j).

objection is not valid, he or she must so notify the individual, who then has the right to place a statement on the basis for the objection in his or her file.[48]

If the person seeking an administrative remedy is not satisfied with the holder's response to the letter of objection, he or she can appeal the agency's decision. The letter of appeal and request for a hearing must be filed within 30 days of the decision. The agency must then hold a hearing within 30 days. After the hearing, the agency has 7 days to write to the person who appealed, stating the decision, the reasons supporting the decision, and the opportunity for further review.[49]

If, after the hearing, a person is still not satisfied with the decision, further review is available from the applicable cabinet secretary.[50] One has 30 days after receiving notice of the hearing decision to send a letter to the secretary asking for further review. The secretary must review all of the previous actions and follow specified procedures in reaching a decision. The secretary's decision is the final step in the administrative appeal process. If a decision at any stage of the administrative appeal process is not reached within the specified time period, regulations provide that the person appealing the case automatically wins by default.[51]

---

48. *Id.*
49. *Id.*
50. 801 CMR 3.04.
51. *Id.*

Practice Related to the Law

Families and Juveniles

5A.1

Competency to Marry

Massachusetts law provides that persons under 18 years of age cannot marry without a parent's or guardian's consent.[1] If a minor marries before the age of majority the minor is considered emancipated[2] from his or her parents. In some states, MHPs are asked to consider whether certain persons are competent to marry. In Massachusetts, such determinations occur only indirectly, in guardianship or similar proceedings. In the absence of a person being under guardianship, one is considered competent to marry.

---

1. Mass. Gen. L. ch. 207, § 25.
2. Mass. Gen. L. ch. 231, § 85P.

5A.2

Guardianship for Adults

Guardianship is the broadest and most restrictive form of decision-making help. A guardian is someone appointed by the probate and family court to handle *both* the personal and financial affairs of another person (the *ward*) who, due to mental retardation, mental illness, or certain other conditions, is incapable of handling his or her own affairs.[1] These functions can be split between two or more guardians.

Guardianship is appropriate for persons with very serious problems of judgment or intellectual capacity due to mental illness or mental retardation. It is also appropriate for persons who are unable to function independently. There must be a serious risk to the individual's health, life, or safety.[2] Guardianship is not intended to protect a person from normal daily risks and should not be used simply because someone is about to make decisions that show poor judgment. An example of a significant threat to a person's welfare is if he or she needs medical treatment but is incapable of signing the necessary consent forms. However, refusal of treatment is not per se cause for guardianship unless the person, by virtue of mental illness, cannot understand the consequences of such refusal. MHPs are often asked to evaluate persons for possible guardianships.

---

1. Mass. Gen. L. ch. 201, §§ 6 and 6A.
2. 104 CMR 15.03 (10).

Who May Seek Appointment of a Guardian

Mental Illness

A mentally ill person suffers from a substantial disorder of thought, mood, or perception that creates a very substantial risk of harm to self or others.[3] A parent, two or more relatives or friends, a Massachusetts nonprofit corporation authorized to act as a guardian of a mentally ill person, or the Department of Mental Health may seek to have a guardian appointed for the mentally ill person.[4]

Mental Retardation

A person who has a permanent condition affecting learning capacity is mentally retarded.[5] A parent, two or more relatives or friends, a Massachusetts nonprofit corporation "whose corporate charter authorizes the corporation to act as guardian for a mentally retarded person," or any agency within the Executive Office of Human Services or Educational Affairs is eligible to seek guardianship.[6]

Spendthriftness

A *spendthrift* is defined as a "person who, by excessive drinking, gaming, idleness, or debauchery of any kind, so spends, wastes or lessens his estate as to expose himself or his family to want or suffering, or the department of public welfare to charge or expense for his support or for the support of his family."[7] The Department of Public Welfare or a relative may bring a petition for appointment of this type of guardian.

Physical Incapacitation or Illness

This new category for guardianship has the same requirements for appointment as those for mental illness.[8]

Filing the Petition

A petition is filed in probate and family court in the county where the proposed ward is an inhabitant or resides, or if he or she lives

---

3. 104 CMR 2.02.
4. Mass. Gen. L. ch. 201, § 6.
5. 104 CMR 20.02 (48).
6. Mass. Gen. L. ch. 201, § 6A.
7. Mass. Gen. L. ch. 201, § 8.
8. Mass. Gen. L. ch. 201, § 6B, added by St. 1990, ch. 149.

outside Massachusetts, in the county where he or she has property.[9] If the ward is from out of state but currently resides in an institution or facility in Massachusetts, venue lies in the county where the facility or institution is located.

Notice

At least 7 days' notice is required of the time and place of the hearing on a petition to appoint a guardian for an alleged mentally ill or retarded person. Notice must be given to the person; the Department of Mental Health; the United States Veterans Administration, if the person is entitled to any veterans' benefits; and "heirs apparent or presumptive," including husband or wife, if any.[10] In the case of an alleged spendthrift, notice must be given to the person and, if a married woman, to her husband.

Other Requirements

Concerning a mentally ill person, the court may require the proposed ward to submit to an examination of his or her mental condition; it may also appoint one or more physicians to examine the proposed ward and report their conclusions to the court. If the court is requested to authorize admission of the proposed ward to a mental health or retardation facility, it must hold a hearing and provide counsel for the ward if the ward is indigent. The court shall also require that the ward attend such a hearing unless "extraordinary circumstances require his absence." A guardian is only authorized to approve psychotropic medication or electroconvulsive therapy or to admit the ward to a mental health facility if specifically authorized by a court.[11]

For the mentally retarded person, the petition must be accompanied by a clinical team report of a social worker, psychologist, and physician indicating that the proposed ward is retarded to such a degree that he or she is incapable of handling his or her affairs. The court may order a mental status examination. As with allegedly mentally ill persons, the court must hold a hearing and provide counsel for the ward if it is requested to authorize the ward's admission to a mental health or mental retardation facility.

---

9. Mass. Gen. L. ch. 201, §§ 7 and 9.
10. *Id.*
11. Rogers v. Commissioner of the Department of Mental Health, 390 Mass. 489, 458 N.E.2d 308 (1983).

Legal Standards for Appointment of a Guardian

Mentally Ill Person

The court must find that the person "is incapable of taking care of himself by reason of mental illness." Regulations of the Department of Mental Health define *mental illness* as a substantial disorder of thought, mood, or perception that creates a substantial risk of harm to self or others, or a risk to the person of inability to care for his- or herself. In each case, the risk must be substantial and immediate.[12]

Mentally Retarded Person

The court must find that:[13]

1. the person is so disabled by mental retardation as to be incapable of making informed decisions about personal and financial affairs;

2. failure to appoint a guardian would create an unreasonable risk to the person's health, welfare, and property; and

3. appointing a conservator with power only over the property of the ward and not the ward's personal affairs would not eliminate such risk.

Spendthrift

The court must find, after a hearing, that the person is a *spendthrift* in accordance with the statutory definition.

Duties of the Guardian

In all four cases of a mentally ill, physically incapacitated, mentally retarded, or spendthrift ward, a permanent guardian is appointed as "guardian of [the ward's] person and estate."[14] Accordingly, the guardian makes all important personal and financial decisions for the ward relating to shelter and food, welfare aid, legal assistance, debts, expenditures, and more. The court may restrict the terms of a guardianship and place limitations on the guardian's power.[15] The probate court is empowered to tailor a guardianship plan ac-

---

12. 104 CMR 3.09.
13. Mass. Gen. L. ch. 201, § 6A.
14. Mass. Gen. L. ch. 201, §§ 6, 6A, and 8.
15. Guardianship of Bassett, 7 Mass. App. Ct. 56, 385 N.E.2d 1024 (1979).

cording to the actual needs of the ward. Thus, the power of the guardian can be limited to situations where the ward actually requires assistance.[16] As noted earlier, to approve certain treatments or admission to a mental health facility, the guardian must be specifically empowered by a court. The mere fact that a person is under guardianship does not authorize the guardian to approve intrusive treatment or psychotropic medications.[17] Guardianship may overcome refusal of psychotropic medication if the hospital or other petitioner proves beyond a reasonable doubt that the ward should have the medication.[18] When such an order is approved, the ward is entitled to annual review of the order.[19] (For more on the duties of a guardian, see Chapter 5A.3.)

In the case of a spendthrift, if a petition to appoint a guardian is recorded and granted, it voids all contracts involving land and all gifts, sales, or transfers of personal property unless approved by the court.[20] The court may authorize the conveyance of land or payment from the personal estate of the ward to his or her spouse, children, or grandchildren.[21]

Commitment of the Ward to an Institution

The guardian of a mentally ill or mentally retarded person may not commit his or her ward to an institution without specific court approval after a hearing where the ward must be represented by counsel.[22] To authorize the guardian of a mentally ill or mentally retarded person to commit the ward to an institution, the judge must find beyond a reasonable doubt that commitment is in the best interest of the ward.[23]

Effect of Guardianship

The ward loses many civil and legal rights, e.g., the right to vote, to make contracts, to make major expenditures without the guardian's consent, and to sign Social Security checks. The right to marry or to make a will is not automatically denied. If specifically authorized, the guardian's authority may also include consent to give or withhold certain medical treatment.[24]

---

16. *Id.*
17. Rogers v. Commissioner of the Department of Mental Health, 390 Mass. 489, 458 N.E.2d 308 (1983).
18. *Id.*
19. Guardianship of Weedon, 409 Mass. 196, 565 N.E.2d 432 (1991).
20. Mass. Gen. L. ch. 201, § 10.
21. *Id.*
22. In re Roe III, 383 Mass. 414, 421 N.E.2d 40 (1981).
23. Doe v. Doe, 377 Mass. 272, 385 N.E.2d 995 (1979).
24. Superintendent of Belchertown State School v. Saikewicz, 373 Mass. 728, 370 N.E.2d 417 (1977).

Termination, Removal, or Substitution of Guardianship

The probate court may terminate a guardianship "upon application of the ward or otherwise, when it appears that the guardianship is no longer necessary."[25] In the case of a mentally ill person, 7 days' notice of the petition by the ward must be given to the Department of Mental Health.[26]

Temporary Guardians

Eligibility and Appointment

Temporary guardians are intended only for emergency situations where there is no time to satisfy the notice requirements and procedural protections associated with petitions for permanent guardianship. Accordingly, the law[27] requires that a decree or order appointing a temporary guardian indicate "the nature of the emergency requiring such appointment and the particular harm sought to be avoided" and specifically limit the temporary guardian's authority to actions reasonably necessary to deal with the emergency.[28]

Temporary guardianship is usually an interim step before permanent guardianship and lasts for 90 days. At the end of 90 days, the temporary guardianship will end unless extended or converted into a permanent guardianship.[29] Nevertheless, a temporary guardian is empowered to carry out his or her duties to their fullest extent notwithstanding any appeal taken from the appointment, unless the Supreme Judicial Court orders otherwise.[30] The appointment of a permanent guardian also terminates a temporary guardianship, as does any order of or discharge by the probate court.[31]

Guardian ad Litem

In any proceeding for guardianship, the court may appoint a guardian ad litem. The guardian ad litem may act as the ward's

---

25. Mass. Gen. L. ch. 201, § 13.
26. Mass. Gen. L. ch. 201, § 13A.
27. Mass. Gen. L. ch. 201, § 14.
28. *Id.*
29. *See* Probate Court R. 29B.
30. Mass. Gen. L. ch. 201, § 14.
31. *Id.*

representative during the legal proceeding.[32] More commonly, the guardian ad litem will act as either an investigator to report to the court or as an evaluator to make a recommendation concerning competency.[33] MHPs are frequently asked to be guardians ad litem in the evaluator role. A judge has inherent authority and discretion on whether to appoint a guardian ad litem and on what responsibility to give the guardian ad litem.[34]

Protection of Religious Practice

A new statute requires guardians to protect their wards' freedom of religion and religious practice.[35]

---

32. Mass. Gen. L. ch. 201, § 34.
33. Matter of Spring, 380 Mass. 629, 405 N.E.2d 115 (1980).
34. Superintendent of Belchertown State School v. Saikewicz, 373 Mass. 728, 370 N.E.2d 417 (1977).
35. Mass. Gen. L. ch. 201, § 51, added by St. 1990, ch. 397.

5A.3

Conservatorship for Adults

Conservatorship is a more limited form of supervision than guardianship. A conservator has power only over the property of his or her ward, not the ward's person.[1] Thus, the ward of a conservator remains free to make his or her own personal decisions, including medical decisions. MHPs are required to evaluate potential wards for incompetence for involuntary conservatorship and for competency for voluntary conservatorship. Eligibility for appointment as conservator varies according to the person for whom it is sought.

Who May Seek Appointment of a Conservator

Advanced Age or Mental Illness

In the case of a person who "by reason of advanced age or mental weakness is unable to properly care for his property," a petition seeking appointment of a conservator may be brought by the person or by one or more of his or her friends or family members.[2]

Physical Incapacity

The petition for appointment of a conservator for a person unable to care for his or her property because of physical incapacity must be brought by the proposed ward or with the ward's consent.[3]

---

1. Mass. Gen. L. ch. 201, § 16.
2. *Id.*
3. *Id.*

Mental Retardation

A petition for appointment of a conservator may be brought by a parent of a mentally retarded person, a Massachusetts nonprofit corporation authorized to act as a conservator of a mentally retarded person, or any agency within the Executive Office of Human Services (e.g., Department of Public Welfare, Department of Mental Health).[4]

Notice and Hearing

The court must hold a hearing on every petition for appointment of a conservator. Normally, at least 7 days' notice must be given to the proposed ward unless the court directs shorter notice for cause shown.[5] Notice must also be given to the heirs and spouse, if any, of the proposed ward and the United States Veterans Administration if the ward is entitled to veterans benefits.

Clinical Team Report

In the case of a mentally retarded person, a clinical team composed of a physician, psychologist, and social worker must examine the proposed ward and make a report. The clinical team report must conclude that the person is mentally retarded to such a degree that he or she is incapable of making informed decisions with respect to the conduct of his or her financial affairs.[6]

Legal Standards for Appointment of a Conservator

Advanced Age or Mental Weakness

A conservator may be appointed for a person of *advanced age* or *mental weakness* if the court finds that the person is "unable to properly care for his property."[7]

Physical Incapacity

Physical incapacity may be a reason for appointing a conservator. However, the proposed ward must request or agree to the appointment.[8]

---

4. Mass. Gen. L. ch. 201, § 17.
5. *Id.*
6. Mass. Gen. L. ch. 201, § 16B.
7. Mass. Gen. L. ch. 201, § 16.
8. *Id.*

Mental Retardation

For a mentally retarded person,[9] the court must find that: (a) the person "is incapable of making informed decisions with respect to the conduct of financial affairs," and (b) failure to appoint a conservator will create an unreasonable risk to the person's property.

Power and Duties of the Conservator

Handles Financial Affairs

The conservator is to handle the ward's financial affairs in the best interest of the ward.[10] The conservator thus shares the responsibility for the ward's life with the ward. The conservator handles only financial matters, while the ward makes his or her own personal decisions.

Manages for the Benefit of Ward

An important obligation, which holds for guardians as well, is to manage the ward's estate for the benefit of the ward rather than for the sake of future heirs or for the conservator's own convenience.[11] In some cases the ward's estate, if sufficiently large, can be partially used for support and maintenance of needy dependents. Again, certain decisions are considered sufficiently serious to require special court authorization: selling real estate, making substantial gifts, or dispersing assets for tax purposes.

Legal Actions

The conservator, in addition to making financial decisions, is responsible for initiating or responding to any legal actions concerning debts owed to or by the ward.[12] The same is true for a guardian.

Exempted Funds

In the case of a mentally retarded ward, the law allows for up to $300 per month to be exempt from the conservatorship and left to the ward to handle.[13] This exemption could probably be requested for mentally ill wards as well, as long as the ward could handle the money responsibly.

---

9. Mass. Gen. L. ch. 201, § 16B.
10. Mass. Gen. L. ch. 201, § 20.
11. *Id.*
12. *Id.*
13. Mass. Gen. L. ch. 201, § 16B.

Temporary Conservatorship

A temporary conservator may be appointed, with or without notice, after petition by the same persons that may apply for appointment of a permanent conservator. A temporary conservator has the same powers and duties as a permanent conservator so far as applicable.[14]

---

14. Mass. Gen. L. ch. 201, § 20.

5A.4

Annulment

While a divorce dissolves what was once a valid, functioning marriage, annulment is the legal process whereby a marriage is declared void and is deemed never to have existed.[1]

Grounds for Annulment

Massachusetts law does not set forth specific grounds for annulment but treats the matter as if a contract for marriage existed but is voided. A marriage may be annulled when one of the parties at the initiation of the marriage intentionally misrepresents or conceals a material fact so that the other person's reason for entering the marriage is defeated.[2]

Annulment of a marriage is commonly sought by and granted to parents of underage minors who run off to get married. Marriages may also be annulled if one or both parties were mentally incompetent.[3] The procedures for obtaining an annulment are the same as those for the dissolution of marriage.[4] (See Chapter 5A.5.) MHPs are sometimes asked to evaluate persons who wish to annul a marriage.

---

1. Calloway v. Thomas, 322 Mass. 580, 78 N.E.2d 637 (1948).
2. Reynolds v. Reynolds, 85 Mass. 605 (1862).
3. Mass. Gen. L. ch. 207, § 16.
4. *Id.*

5A.5

Divorce

Before 1975, divorce law in Massachusetts required the petitioning party to allege fault by the other spouse. This changed when Massachusetts adopted the *no-fault* concept for divorce. No-fault law authorizes divorce for the irretrievable breakdown of a marriage either with or without a separation agreement.[1] Litigation then centers around property division, child support, spousal maintenance, or child custody. MHPs may contribute to this process by evaluating one or both parties to the divorce or the children.

Divorce Procedure

The dissolution of marriage is initiated by a complaint brought in probate and family court.[2] The complaint must allege and satisfy three threshold requirements. First, one of the parties must have been domiciled in Massachusetts for 12 months prior to the filing of the petition. Second, the marriage must not be amenable to conciliation. The court may order or the parties may seek counseling assistance through the court's probation office (family service office). This process consists of individual meetings between a counselor and each of the parties. Referrals may be made to professional specialists in the mental health field or other services. All dissolution proceedings are stayed upon the parties entering counseling. Counseling is not necessary where it would be useless. Third, the complaint must allege that the marriage is irretrievably broken.

---

1. Mass. Gen. L. ch. 208, §§ 1A and 1B.
2. *Id.*

There is no legal test to determine whether there has been an irreparable break. The parties must attest by affidavit that the marriage is beyond repair.

Upon a finding that the marriage should be dissolved, the court will make provisions for division of property, support payments, and child custody (see Chapter 5A.6). (The court looks to the parties to divide the assets of the marriage. When the parties cannot agree, they can litigate disputed matters.) These matters are incorporated into a decree of divorce that becomes final 90 days after it is entered if based on irretrievable breakdown or 30 days after for other grounds.[3]

With regard to child support payments and alimony, the court may issue an order or accept the agreement of the parties. The complaint for divorce must be accompanied by financial information about both parties, if possible, or at least financial information about the plaintiff.[4]

The probate and family court has adopted child support guidelines. These are mathematical calculations designed to determine the amount of child support to be paid. Wherever possible, the court will apply these guidelines to determine child support. The decision to award child support is supposed to be gender neutral.[5]

Although their use has declined in recent years, fault grounds for divorce still exist. They include cruel and abusive treatment, desertion, impotence, and adultery.[6] In a fault divorce, the plaintiff alleges that the basis for the divorce is one or more of the fault grounds. MHPs may be called to testify in fault divorces alleging abuse. Fault divorces are used when the parties cannot agree to a no-fault divorce, because a no-fault divorce brought by only one spouse, rather than by mutual agreement, cannot be heard by the probate court for 6 months.[7] Financial awards should not be affected by whether the divorce is granted on fault or no-fault grounds.

Massachusetts is an equitable-division-of-property state. Property is divided according to the length of the marriage and the respective contributions and needs of the parties.[8]

---

3. Mass. Gen. L. ch. 208, § 34.
4. Form CJ-D 301; Appendix to Mass. R. Dom. Rel. P.
5. Form CJ-D 304; Appendix to Mass. R. Dom. Rel. P.
6. Mass. Gen. L. ch. 208, § 2.
7. Mass. Gen. L. ch. 208, § 1B.
8. Mass. Gen. L. ch. 208, § 34.

5A.6

Child Custody After Marital Dissolution

Child custody determinations can result from four types of changes in the legal status of a marriage: annulment, separate support, divorce, or modification of a divorce decree. MHPs may become involved in a child custody determination in one of two ways. First, a party may request an MHP to conduct an evaluation of a parent's, proposed custodial parent's, or child's mental status and to testify as an expert witness. Second, an MHP who has provided services to the family unit, whether diagnostic or therapeutic, may be subpoenaed by either party to present evidence as a witness. MHPs may also be involved in child custody disputes arising from paternity actions.

Criteria to Establish Court Jurisdiction

The authority of the court to assume jurisdiction over the child is generally a factual determination based on the domicile of the child and parents. For instance, if a child is living in Massachusetts at the commencement of a divorce proceeding, the court automatically assumes jurisdiction. If, however, the child and the parents are not domiciled in the Commonwealth, then three criteria must be met for the court to assume jurisdiction. The court must determine that (a) it is in the best interests of the child for the court to assume jurisdiction; (b) the child and at least one parent have significant connections with Massachusetts; and (c) there is sufficient evidence in the Commonwealth concerning the child's present or future care, protection, and upbringing.[1] In this situation, an

---

1. Mass. Gen. L. ch. 209B, § 2.

MHP may be asked to testify concerning the nature and quality of the child's relationships with persons in Massachusetts, as well as the advisability of a Massachusetts court assuming jurisdiction compared to a court in the state where the child resides. Massachusetts subscribes to the Uniform Child Custody Jurisdiction Act, which requires a Massachusetts judge to determine whether the court here or a court in another state should assume jurisdiction based on the same factors described above.[2]

The Standard in Custody Determinations: Best Interests of the Child

The court determines custody in accordance with the best interests of the child. In deciding what that constitutes, the court may consider all relevant factors. There is no prescription either for or against shared custody.[3] If shared custody is desired, the parties are encouraged to present a shared custody plan for consideration by the court.[4] An award of shared legal or physical custody does not affect obligations for child support.[5]

A parent not granted custody of a child is entitled to reasonable visitation rights unless the court finds, after a hearing, that visitation would seriously endanger the child's physical, mental, moral, or emotional health.[6] The court will consider the same factors used in the custody determination to decide reasonable visitation rights; there are no preset formulas or guidelines. The testimony of MHPs concerning the mental health of a child and how that would be affected by a particular plan for custody is often critical to the decision-making process. MHPs may be asked to evaluate whether the child was abused by one or both of the parents.[7]

Mental Status Evaluation: Mandatory and Voluntary

The probate court may authorize an examination into the mental health of a party where it is demonstrated that the "mental . . .

---

2. Mass. Gen. L. ch. 209B.
3. Mass. Gen. L. ch. 208, § 31.
4. Mass. Gen. L. ch. 208, § 31, as amended by St. 1989, ch. 689.
5. Id.
6. Mass. Gen. L. ch. 208, § 31.
7. LaLonde v. LaLonde, 30 Mass. App. Ct. 117, 566 N.E.2d 620 (1991).

condition . . . of a party, or of a person in custody or under legal control of a party, is in controversy."[8] Mental status evaluations may also be conducted on a voluntary basis. This usually occurs where one of the parties requests an MHP to undertake an evaluation of the children's parents. If the other party does not wish to participate in the evaluation, the court cannot order the person to do so. The testimony of an MHP is advisory only; the court is not bound to follow it.[9]

Confidentiality and Privileged Communications

In the majority of examinations, the information obtained by a psychologist, psychiatrist, or social worker is confidential (see Chapter 4.2) and privileged (see Chapter 4.3). Where the psychologist, psychiatrist, or social worker conducts an evaluation under court order, an exception to privilege applies because the evaluation is being performed on behalf of the court.[10] Nonetheless, it is good practice for an MHP to obtain a written authorization from the party being evaluated to release any information pertaining to the court-ordered evaluation before it is commenced.

A complicated situation arises where an MHP has provided services to both the husband and wife as a couple. Under the recent amendment to the psychotherapist privilege statute extending it to marital and family therapy, it is now clear that such communications are privileged unless *both* parties waive the privilege.[11]

Because custody determinations are based in large part on the testimony of MHPs, they should be prepared to testify whenever they have seen a divorcing person in therapy. MHPs must obtain waivers of privilege in such circumstances.

Paternity Actions

Massachusetts has an elaborate system for determining paternity and awarding custody and support.[12] Generally, a child born to an unmarried woman has the same rights as a child born to a married couple who are divorcing. Thus, the child support requirements are identical. Once paternity is established by blood or genetic marker testing or acknowledged by the father, the court may award custody and visitation to the appropriate person. If custody is contested, the testimony of an MHP as to parental fitness is

---

8. Mass. R. Dom. Rel. P. 35 (a).
9. *Id.*
10. Mass. Gen. L. ch. 233, § 20B; Mass. Gen. L. ch. 135, § 135A.
11. Mass. Gen. L. ch. 233, § 20B.
12. Mass. Gen. L. ch. 209C.

generally required.[13] In order to establish paternity, a court may order the mother, child, and the putative father to submit to a blood or genetic marker test.[14]

13. Mass. Gen. L. ch. 209C, § 3.
14. Mass. Gen. L. ch. 209, § 17, as amended by St. 1990, ch. 437.

5A.7

Reporting of Adult Abuse

The law[1] requires MHPs to report known or suspected abuse, neglect, or exploitation of patients at hospitals or nursing homes. It is a mandatory reporting law that carries criminal sanctions for noncompliance.[2] Failure to follow the law may also result in civil liability from suits brought by the adults the law is designed to protect. In addition, persons abused in a family or dating situation may obtain protection from the courts. The statute was created to prevent domestic abuse of all kinds. It allows an abused person to bring a cause of action by completing a simple petition and appearing ex parte before a judge.[3]

Terms and Definitions

Abuse is defined as the nonaccidental infliction of physical or emotional injury. *Neglect* is the failure to provide adequate food, shelter, or clothing. Forcing an adult to submit to the will of another is *exploitation*.[4]

Who Must Report

The statute requires all MHPs to report cases of suspected abuse in health institutions (hospitals or nursing homes) to the Depart-

---

1. Mass. Gen. L. ch. 111, §§ 72G–72J; *see also* 651 CMR 5.02.
2. *Id.*
3. Mass. Gen. L. ch. 209A, as amended by St. 1990, ch. 403.
4. Mass. Gen. L. ch. 111, §§ 72G–72J; *see also* 651 CMR 5.02.

ment of Public Health.[5] If the Department of Public Health supports the allegation, it can offer services.

How a Household Abuse Report is Filed

The statute is designed to operate simply. The allegedly abused person fills out a simple form in district, probate, or superior court and may obtain a 5-day temporary order after a brief hearing. The temporary order must be served on the offender by a police officer. The order may require the person to vacate the house, award temporary custody of children, or require the offender to stay away from the victim. A restraining order against an offender may be made permanent at a hearing held after the 5-day order expires. If child custody is involved, the case must be brought in probate court.[6] Violation of a restraining order is a criminal offense.[7]

Family Abuse

A family member or a person in or formerly in a dating relationship alleging actual physical or emotional injury or immediate fear of injury by someone in or formerly in the household—spouse, child, or present or former boyfriend or girlfriend—may seek a restraining order.[8] The adult alleging abuse must be a household member, spouse, child, or blood relative of the abuser,[9] or have a past or present dating relationship with the abuser.[10]

Elder Abuse

MHPs are required to report instances of suspected abuse that come to their attention involving persons over the age of 60 to the Department of Elder Affairs.[11] The reporting requirement applies to all MHPs, and failure to report is a criminal offense.[12] The Department of Elder Affairs investigates reports of abuse and

---

5. *Id.*
6. Mass. Gen. L. ch. 209A, as amended by St. 1990, ch. 403.
7. Mass. Gen. L. ch. 209A, § 8, as amended by St. 1990, ch. 403.
8. Mass. Gen. L. ch. 209A, as amended by St. 1990, ch. 403.
9. *Id.*
10. *Id.*
11. Mass. Gen. L. ch. 19A, § 14; *see also* 651 CMR 5.00 *et seq.*
12. Mass. Gen. L. ch. 19A, § 15.

may authorize protective services to assist the abused person. Assistance may include homework services, emergency shelter, and other help.[13]

Disabled Persons Abuse

MHPs are also required to report instances of suspected abuse of disabled persons that come to their attention to the Disabled Persons Protection Commission. The commission then conducts investigations and offers services.[14]

---

13. Mass. Gen. L. ch. 19A, §§ 16–19.
14. Mass. Gen. L. ch. 19C, § 10.

5A.8

Reporting of Child Abuse

Massachusetts law[1] requires certain professionals having contact with children to report known or suspected incidents of child abuse including neglect and sexual or physical abuse. The statute includes children physically dependent on addictive drugs at birth. The MHP is an integral part of the reporting, investigating, and implementing procedures.[2]

Terms and Definitions

Abuse is defined as the nonaccidental commission of an act by a caretaker that causes or creates a substantial risk of serious physical or emotional injury to a child.[3] Abuse may be physical or sexual. *Neglect* is the intentional withholding of necessary food, clothing, shelter, or medical care.[4]

Who Must Report

The law applies to psychologists, physicians, dentists, osteopaths, chiropractors, podiatrists, nurses, school personnel, social workers, police officers, and any other person having responsibility for the care of children.[5] Since there is no requirement that the MHP be

---

1. Mass. Gen. L. ch. 119, § 51A.
2. Mass. Gen. L. ch. 119, § 51A, as amended by St. 1989, ch. 219.
3. 110 CMR 2.00 (1).
4. 110 CMR 2.00 (35).
5. Mass. Gen. L. ch. 119, § 51A, as amended by St. 1990, § 474.

licensed, all MHPs have a legal duty to report child abuse under this law.

When Must a Report Be Made?

The duty to report applies whenever a mandatory reporter has reasonable cause to believe that a child has suffered abuse.[6] The legislature considered it so important that the Department of Social Services (DSS) be made aware of cases of suspected abuse that it exempted mandatory reporters from liability. Nonmandated persons are also encouraged to report suspicions. As long as a report from a nonmandated person is made in good faith, he or she is protected from civil liability. In addition, the statute protects reporters from being discriminated against in their jobs as a result of reporting.[7]

Reportable abuse or neglect must have been caused by a caretaker such as a parent or teacher.[8] More importantly, the fact that a parent is seeking treatment for a child does not absolve the professional of the duty to report. Rather, the duty to report applies whenever a mandatory reporter learns of abuse or neglect.

How to Report

The duty to report is fulfilled by a telephone call to DSS, which will take down the necessary information. There is a hot line number to make reporting easy. The report must include the names and addresses of the child and the child's parents or of the person or persons having custody of the child, if known; the child's age and the nature and extent of the injuries, including any evidence of previous occurrences; and any other information that the person reporting believes might be helpful in establishing causation. (See also Chapter 5A.9.)

Confidentiality and Privilege

As discussed in Chapter 4.2, the duty to report cases of suspected child abuse is an exception to the general requirement of confidentiality of communications between MHPs and clients.

---

6. *Id.*
7. Mass. Gen. L. ch. 119, § 51A, as amended by St. 1989, ch. 396.
8. 110 CMR 2.00 (17).

Failure to Report

A mandatory reporter who fails to report may be punished by a fine not exceeding $1,000.[9]

---

9. Mass. Gen. L. ch. 119, § 51A.

5A.9

Abused and Neglected Children

Procedures for handling child abuse and neglect cases typically involve three stages: (a) investigation of a complaint by the Department of Social Services (DSS), (b) removal of a minor from home where necessary for safety, and (c) bringing the matter to court for action to protect a child. This process may stop at any point if the allegations are unsupported or on a showing that the parents are currently capable of raising their children in a responsible manner.[1] Each stage may involve a mental health evaluation of the child or parent. In addition, the MHP may be called to testify at the hearing as an expert witness. (See Chapter 5A.10.)

Reporting

Until 1983, the primary focus of legislation pertaining to child abuse in the Commonwealth was to ensure that cases came to the attention of DSS. To do this, the legislature created a mandatory reporting system. This system requires that certain people, including all MHPs, report suspected cases of child abuse or neglect to DSS. Mandated reporters are professionals who the legislature has determined *must* file a report with DSS whenever they have reasonable cause to believe that a child has suffered neglect or abuse.[2] (See Chapter 5A.8.)

In 1983, the legislature amended the child abuse law to provide that DSS must notify the appropriate district attorney's office

---

1. Mass. Gen. L. ch. 119, § 51A; 110 CMR 2.00 (31).
2. *Id.*

whenever a supported child abuse case involves a child who has: (a) died, (b) been raped, (c) suffered brain damage or loss of a bodily function or organ, (d) been sexually exploited, (e) suffered serious bodily injury from a repeated pattern of abuse by a family member, or (f) been subject to an indecent assault and battery.[3]

In addition to notifying the district attorney of the report that DSS receives, the law also requires that DSS provide the district attorney and the local police department with the initial report and its investigation.[4] DSS and the district attorney must then hold a multidisciplinary conference to determine whether a case should be handled criminally or as a child protection matter.[5]

DSS or an MHP may also file a petition for care and protection in the district court. These are civil cases in which the court is asked to determine that a child has been abused or neglected and to authorize services to the child or family. After a hearing, a judge may order appropriate services and, in extreme cases, may transfer custody.[6]

Screening

Once a DSS office hears of abuse or neglect of a child, the report is screened to determine if there is reasonable cause to believe that a child is suffering emotional or physical injury from abuse or neglect.[7] During the screening evaluation, DSS attempts to gather as much identifying information as possible, including the name and age of the child, the child's present location, the names and locations of parents and other siblings, and the names of other professionals who are already involved with the family and who might be of assistance in helping DSS make an informed decision about whether intervention is necessary.

During the screening evaluation, the information that the reporter gave to DSS is closely examined for credibility.[8] As part of the investigation, DSS social workers are expected to view and interview all children reported as having been abused or neglected. An attempt is also made to view other children in the family. Parents are contacted and interviewed. If at the conclusion of the screening interview DSS determines that there is reasonable cause to believe that a child may be at risk, the report is *supported*. DSS will then offer services. A report will be *screened out* when the

---

3. Mass. Gen. L. ch. 119, § 51D.
4. Mass. Gen. L. ch. 119, § 51B (3).
5. Mass. Gen. L. ch. 119, § 51B, as amended by St. 1989, ch. 561.
6. Mass. Gen. L. ch. 119, § 23.
7. 110 CMR 4.00.
8. *See* Mass. Gen. L. ch. 119, §§ 51A and 51B.

information gathered during the screening evaluation does not provide reasonable cause to believe that a child is suffering serious physical or emotional injury from abuse or neglect.[9] This initial assessment is an attempt by DSS to responsibly protect children who may be at risk while also respecting the integrity of families. The initial evaluation must be completed in 10 days.[10]

When a report is accepted, DSS must decide whether it warrants an emergency or a nonemergency response. DSS must determine whether the situation as reported poses a threat of immediate danger to the life, health, or physical safety of the child. In an emergency investigation, DSS is supposed to respond within 24 hours.[11]

Voluntary Services

When a report is not supported but it appears that a family could benefit from services by DSS, the agency may offer voluntary services to the family.[12] Such services could include day care, counseling, homemaker, and chore services. The family can accept or reject the services.

Care and Protection

If voluntary services are insufficient or unaccepted, DSS may seek coercive action through a care and protection proceeding.[13] After a court petition is filed, the court will appoint an investigator to recommend whether intervention is required and, if so, what services should be provided. The standard for intervention is parental unfitness that is proven by clear and convincing evidence.[14]

The law also mandates that DSS maintain a central registry of names of supported cases under strict requirements of confidentiality.[15] Names in the central registry include perpetrators of abuse and the names of children from supported cases. Names of children remain in the central registry until a child is age 18 or a younger sibling turns 18 years old.

---

9. 110 CMR 4.32.
10. Mass. Gen. L. ch. 119, § 51B.
11. *Id.*
12. 110 CMR 4.01.
13. Mass. Gen. L. ch. 119, §§ 23–27; Care and Protection of Zelda, 26 Mass. App. Ct. 809, 534 N.E.2d 7 (1989).
14. Custody of a Minor (No. 2), 368 Mass. 741, 438 N.E.2d 38 (1982).
15. Mass. Gen. L. ch. 119, §§ 51E and 51F.

DSS has an administrative procedure whereby alleged perpetrators may seek review by a hearing officer of the determination that a report is supported and that an alleged perpetrator's name should be in the central registry.[16] Decisions of the hearing officer may be appealed to the commissioner of DSS and then to the court.[17]

Trial of Abuse Cases

As a result of mandatory reporting and mandatory referral to the district attorney of supported allegations of sexual abuse, there has been a substantial increase in the number of prosecutions of alleged abusers.[18] These cases have engendered unique issues for MHPs.

Because many of the victims and witnesses have been young children, the legislature has attempted to make it easier for children to testify. Most of these efforts have failed. For example, a statute permitting child abuse cases to be tried in a closed courtroom with the public excluded was declared unconstitutional by the United States Supreme Court.[19] Similarly, a statute permitting a child to testify by videotape where the defendant was not present during the videotaping of the child has also been declared unconstitutional.[20] In both cases, the sixth amendment to the U.S. Constitution, which assures defendants in criminal cases the right to confront their accusers, precluded the steps from being taken. The legislature has recently enacted a statute permitting out-of-court statements of children under 10 years of age to be admitted if the child is unable to testify. It is unclear whether this statute will be upheld.[21]

The court has allowed use of videotape testimony where the child testified in the presence of the defendant and the videotape was clear and showed both the witness and the defendant.[22] Further, it is permissible for judges to make the courtroom more pleasant for children victims and witnesses by allowing them to sit at a small table or bring a favorite toy with them.[23]

The basic issue with children victims and witnesses is how to determine their credibility. The child must demonstrate that he or

---

16. 110 CMR 10.00.
17. 110 CMR 10.35.
18. Middlesex County Child Abuse Project, THE CHILD ABUSE REPORTING LAW 5 (1986).
19. Globe Newspaper Co. v. Superior Court, 457 U.S. 596 (1982).
20. Commonwealth v. Bergstrom, 402 Mass. 534, 524 N.E.2d 366 (1989).
21. Mass. Gen. L. ch. 233, §§ 81 and 82, added by St. 1990, ch. 339.
22. Commonwealth v. Tufts, 405 Mass. 610, 542 N.E.2d 586 (1989).
23. Commonwealth v. Amirault, 404 Mass. 221, 535 N.E.2d 193 (1989).

she understands the difference between truthful and untruthful statements and that he or she understands the importance of telling the truth.[24] If a child refuses to cooperate or loses attention, a judge may continue the case to give the child an opportunity to recover his or her attention.[25] However, if the child totally refuses to cooperate on cross-examination, the defendant is entitled to a mistrial because his or her confrontation rights have been violated.[26]

A defendant being prosecuted for abuse is entitled to have the judge examine the records of testifying MHPs to determine whether there is anything in the records that may be helpful to the defense.[27] If the judge determines that such evidence exists, the prosecutor must make them available to the defense.[28] The court order provides an exception to any privilege. (See Chapter 4.3.)

The court will appoint an investigator to report at trial about the child and the family situation.[29] The report of the investigator is admissible even though it contains hearsay resulting from the investigator's discussions with others.[30]

Finally, the Massachusetts Supreme Judicial Court has specifically upheld the use of MHPs as experts in sexual abuse prosecutions to explain to the jury what behavioral or other changes in a child are consistent with having been abused.[31]

---

24. Commonwealth v. Corbett, 26 Mass. App. Ct. 773, 533 N.E.2d 207 (1989).
25. Id.
26. Commonwealth v. Kirouac, 405 Mass. 557, 542 N.E.2d 270 (1989).
27. Pennsylvania v. Ritchie, 480 U.S. 39 (1987).
28. Commonwealth v. Jones, 404 Mass. 339, 535 N.E.2d 221 (1989).
29. Mass. Gen. L. ch. 119, § 24.
30. Custody of Michel, 28 Mass. App. Ct. 260, 549 N.E.2d 440 (1990).
31. Commonwealth v. Dockham, 405 Mass. 618, 542 N.E.2d 591 (1989).

5A.10

Termination of Parental Rights

After a case of suspected child abuse or neglect has been reported and after the Massachusetts Department of Social Services (DSS) has made an investigation, and usually after a care and protection proceeding has been held (see Chapter 5A.9), DSS will sometimes seek authority from a court to terminate parental rights. This is an extreme measure reflecting serious family problems. MHPs are usually involved in these cases, which evaluate the fitness of biological parents to retain their children.

Petition for Termination

Petition Requirements

Any person, agency, or corporation that has a legitimate interest in the welfare of a child may file a petition for the termination of a parent–child relationship.[1] This includes professionals working with a child as well as relatives and other interested persons. As a matter of practice, DSS will usually be the petitioner.

For parental rights to be terminated, the petitioner must prove that the parents are unable to care for the child due to either (a) unavailability,[2] which can be from physical absence, or lack of present ability to care for a specific child; or (b) the best interests of the child[3] argue against the child remaining in contact with the parents. The legal standard under Massachusetts law is *current*

---

1. Mass. Gen. L. ch. 119, § 29.
2. Mass. Gen. L. ch. 119, § 23A.
3. Mass. Gen. L. ch. 210, § 3.

unfitness at the time of trial.[4] In the court proceeding, the burden of proof is on the petitioner (usually DSS) to demonstrate a compelling need for the termination of the rights of the natural parents or other caretakers. The probate and family court has exclusive jurisdiction in termination of parental rights cases.[5]

Pre-Hearing Requirements

After a petition has been filed, the court must give notice to the parents and any other interested parties. Where termination is sought, the court must institute safeguards to protect the rights of the child. It may also appoint a guardian ad litem to investigate the situation and report to the court. A guardian ad litem acts as an officer of the court who is authorized to interview relevant persons before reporting to the court. MHPs are sometimes appointed as guardians ad litem. If the case is contested, the court must appoint counsel for the child.[6]

Although the rights of the parents are to be protected, the welfare of the child is the court's paramount consideration. The testimony of MHPs on parental unfitness or the best interests of the child is often crucial in the decision-making process. A judge authorizing the termination of parental rights must write specific and detailed findings justifying termination.[7] The judge may use a family's prior history of unfitness for prognostic effect.[8]

Termination of Parental Rights

The legal standard underlying cases of this type is whether the natural parents are currently fit to further the welfare and best interests of the child.[9] Both the fitness of the parents and the needs of the particular child must be examined. The fact that a child will suffer harm by being returned to the natural parent is not necessarily sufficient to support termination of parental rights.[10] Impact of return on a child is not irrelevant but cannot alone support a

---

4. Petition of the Department of Social Services to Dispense with Consent to Adoption, 397 Mass. 659, 493 N.E.2d 197 (1986); In re Adoption of George, 27 Mass. App. Ct. 265, 537 N.E.2d 1251 (1989).
5. Mass. Gen. L. ch. 210, § 3.
6. Mass. Gen. L. ch. 210, § 3(b).
7. Petition of the Department of Public Welfare to Dispense with Consent to Adoption, 383 Mass. 573, 421 N.E.2d 28 (1981).
8. Petition of the Catholic Charitable Bureau to Dispense with Consent to Adoption, 395 Mass. 180, 479 N.E.2d 148 (1985).
9. Petition of the Department of Social Services to Dispense with Consent to Adoption, 389 Mass. 793, 452 N.E.2d 497 (1983); Adoption of Christine, 405 Mass. 602, 542 N.E.2d 582 (1989).
10. Petition of the Department of Social Services to Dispense with Consent to Adoption, 391 Mass. 113, 461 N.E.2d 186 (1984).

decision to terminate parental rights.[11] Rather, the predicted unfitness of the parents must also be analyzed. The testimony of MHPs is critical to this process.[12] Information that would otherwise be privileged will be admitted into evidence on grounds of best interests of the child, which is an exception to the privilege statutes[13] (see Chapter 4.3).

Conduct and Circumstances That Establish Current Unfitness

A parent who is "disorganized, immature, irresponsible, [and] inconsistent" and whose behavior results in a child being deprived of basic physical and emotional needs is currently unfit.[14] Lack of consistency and responsibility is shown by an inability to maintain steady employment or a stable home environment and by irregularity and unreliability regarding visitation.[15] Other relevant evidence may include the fact that the parent chose inappropriate caretakers; failed to provide the child with a clean, healthy home; did not maintain any sort of financial responsibility; or lacked insight into the child's emotional needs.[16]

Separation from natural parents and bonding with foster parents will only rarely produce a finding of parental unfitness by itself.[17] For a parent's mental disorder to be relevant it must be shown that the disorder has a bearing on the parent's fitness (his or her capacity to assume parental responsibility) or on the child's well-being.[18] Past temporary placements of a child made necessary by physical problems over which the parent had no control would not warrant a finding of unfitness, but a placement because of a parent's emotional problems is relevant to fitness. In addition, failure to cooperate with counseling and treatment is a factor that can be considered. However, failure to get along with a DSS worker is not relevant to fitness.[19]

Custody is not to be transferred from the natural parent simply because another prospective custodian is thought to be better qualified. A pattern of voluntarily placing children in times of stress and then reclaiming them, coupled with an inability to cooperate

---

11. Petition of the Department of Social Services to Dispense with Consent to Adoption, 392 Mass. 696, 467 N.E.2d 861 (1984).
12. Petition of the Catholic Charitable Bureau to Dispense with Consent to Adoption, 392 Mass. 738, 467 N.E.2d 866 (1984).
13. Adoption of Christine, 405 Mass. 602, 542 N.E.2d 582 (1989).
14. Mass. Gen. L. ch. 210, § 3.
15. Care and Protection of Three Minors, 392 Mass. 704, 467 N.E.2d 851 (1984).
16. *Id.*
17. Custody of a Minor, 383 Mass. 595, 421 N.E.2d 63 (1981).
18. Petition of the Department of Social Services to Dispense with Consent to Adoption, 392 Mass. 696, 467 N.E.2d 861 (1984).
19. *Id.*

consistently with service plans, can demonstrate unfitness.[20] Parents cannot be deprived of custody merely because they are poor or choose an unusual lifestyle.[21]

Mere failure to exercise custodial rights in the past (particularly for appropriate reasons) does not support a conclusion of unfitness.[22] Prognostic evidence derived from an ongoing pattern of parental neglect or misconduct may be used to determine future fitness and the likelihood of harm to the child.[23]

Dispositional Orders

The judge must evaluate placement options in light of the best interests of the child.[24]

Visitation After Termination of Parental Rights and Adoption

The trial judge may order postadoptive visitation by parents and perhaps other natural family members if the judge finds this to be in the child's best interests.[25]

Effect of Termination

A termination order removes all of the parent and child relationship except that, in the absence of an adoption order, the child retains inheritance rights.[26] The usual effect of a termination order is to free the child for adoption.

---

20. Petition of Department of Social Services to Dispense with Consent to Adoption, 389 Mass. 793, 452 N.E.2d 497 (1983).
21. Petition of the Department of Public Welfare to Dispense with Consent to Adoption, 383 Mass. 573, 421 N.E.2d 28 (1981).
22. Adoption of Frederick, 405 Mass. 1, 537 N.E.2d 1208 (1989).
23. Custody of a Minor (No. 1), 371 Mass. 572, 463 N.E.2d 324 (1984).
24. Care and Protection of Three Minors, 392 Mass. 704, 467 N.E.2d 851 (1984).
25. Petition of the Department of Social Services to Dispense with Consent to Adoption, 392 Mass. 696, 467 N.E.2d 861 (1984).
26. Mass. Gen. L. ch. 210, § 3.

5A.11

Guardianship for Minors

A guardian may be appointed for a minor in situations where the custodial parent is unable to care for the child due to death, mental illness, or other circumstances that cause the child to be at risk. MHPs are usually involved in such proceedings by giving testimony that evaluates whether the child is at risk unless a guardianship is created.

Application for Guardianship

There are two methods of appointing a guardian for a minor. The first is by testamentary appointment in which the parents indicate in their will whom they wish to be guardian of their children.[1] The second method of appointment is by a formal court hearing that is convened because a person interested in the child's welfare has petitioned the probate and family court to appoint a guardian.[2] This can occur at any time, including at the death of a parent who has not made a testamentary appointment.

The Guardianship Hearing

Petitioners must give notice to the minors if they are over 14 years of age, to the person who has the principal care and custody of the minors, and to any living parent of the minors.[3] At the hearing,

---

1. Mass. Gen. L. ch. 201, § 3.
2. Mass. Gen. L. ch. 201, § 2.
3. *Id.*

the court first determines whether to appoint a guardian. A guardian may be appointed if both parents or a single parent have died without making a testamentary appointment or if parental rights have been terminated or suspended by circumstances or a prior court order.[4]

The court next determines who should be appointed guardian. In considering a given candidate, the court must determine if the appointment would be in the best interests of the minor. The welfare of the child may override presumptions favoring natural parents.[5]

Guardians of minors have the same powers and responsibilities as parents,[6] except that guardians are not legally obligated to provide their own funds for the children and are not liable to third persons for acts of the children.[7] The law[8] further specifies that guardians must:

1. take reasonable care of the children's personal effects;
2. receive money payable for the support of the children;
3. facilitate the children's education and social and other activities; authorize medical or other professional care, treatment, or advice; and consent to marriage or adoption of the children; and
4. report on the condition of the children as specified by court order.

Termination of the Guardianship

A guardian's authority and responsibility terminates on the death, resignation, or removal of the guardian; on the child's death, adoption, or marriage; or when the child reaches 18 years of age.[9] Any person interested in the welfare of the child may petition for removal of the guardian on the ground that removal would be in the best interests of the child. The court will then hold a hearing to determine whether it is in the child's best interests to terminate the guardianship. If so, the court will appoint a new guardian.[10]

---

4. *Id.*
5. *Id.*
6. Mass. Gen. L. ch. 201, § 5.
7. Mass. Gen. L. ch. 201, § 37.
8. Mass. Gen. L. ch. 201, § 2.
9. *Id.*
10. *Id.*

5A.12

Conservatorship for Minors

Whereas guardians are appointed to undertake parental responsibilities for minors when parents are absent or incapacitated (see Chapter 5A.11), conservators are charged with the responsibility of managing or protecting the estates (e.g., money, property, and business enterprises) of minors. There is no requirement that the minor also have a guardian appointed. While it is primarily a financial determination, MHPs may be asked to determine whether minors are capable of handling their estates.

Application for Conservatorship

Any person, including the one to be protected, may petition the probate and family court for the appointment of a conservator. This includes those who would be adversely affected by lack of effective management of the property and affairs, as well as those interested in the person's well-being.[1]

Appointment of a Conservator

The court may appoint a conservator if it determines that the minor has money or owns property that requires management or protection that cannot otherwise be provided. Additionally, the minor may have business affairs that may be jeopardized or prevented by the absence of an adult supervising them, or the minor may

---

1. Mass. Gen. L. ch. 201, § 16.

have funds for support and education that need protection. A conservator may be appointed even though the parents are present and fulfilling the usual parental duties.[2]

Authority and Responsibilities of the Conservator

The court may appoint an individual or a corporation as conservator of the estate. The authority of the conservator is limited to the management of funds.[3]

---

2. *Id.*
3. *Id.*

5A.13

Foster Care

Massachusetts law[1] provides that the Department of Social Services (DSS) may place in foster care children who are not able to live in their own homes. Placement may be short term or long term and is not intended to be a prelude to adoption. MHPs are often asked to evaluate children for placement and prospective foster parents for suitability.

Requirements for Foster Parents

Single or married persons may apply to the Office for Children for approval to provide foster care services.[2] Current state policies favor traditional families and disfavor nontraditional families such as gay couples.[3] Applicants are subject to an interview, a detailed questionnaire, a criminal records check, and a house visit before they are approved to be foster parents.[4] Foster parents are also required to attend an intensive training program. In addition, DSS may visit homes approved by the Office for Children and may remove children in cases where the placement appears inappropriate.[5]

---

1. Mass. Gen. L. ch. 28A, § 10.
2. *Id.*
3. *See* Babets v. Secretary of the Executive Office of Human Services, 403 Mass. 230, 526 N.E.2d 1261 (1988). A challenge to the current state policy is pending.
4. 110 CMR 7.103; Mass. Gen. L. ch. 6, § 172B, added by St. 1990, ch. 319, § 13.
5. Mass. Gen. L. ch. 119, § 22.

Placement of Children in Foster Homes

DSS is responsible for placing children in foster care. The placement may be voluntary or court-ordered.[6] In the case of court-ordered placement, the placement may be short term or it may be in comtemplation of adoption.[7] (See Chapter 5A.10.) Court cases involving involuntary placement of children in foster care are decided on a showing of parental unfitness and a demonstration that the best interests of the child would be served by foster placement.[8] The court may award temporary custody to DSS for the purpose of foster home placement.[9] DSS must have permanent custody before a long-term placement can be offered. Before a child is removed from parents and placed in foster care, the parents are entitled to a full hearing.[10]

In making foster placements, DSS will consider the least restrictive setting for the child; placements that allow contact with the child's family (if applicable); and placements that are with traditional families or families of the same racial, ethnic, or linguistic heritage as the child.[11] DSS regulations require foster care placement with relatives if possible. Foster homes must be clean and safe, and regulations specify conditions for bedrooms, including size.[12] DSS requires training for foster parents and a constant process of evaluation.

When DSS moves to remove a child from foster care, it must give the foster parents reasons for the action.[13] Such actions are subject to administrative hearings and court review. Similarly, in extreme situations, DSS can seek court authority to close a foster home.[14]

---

6. Mass. Gen. L. ch. 119, § 23.
7. *Id.*
8. Custody of a Minor, 21 Mass. App. Ct. 1, 483 N.E.2d 473 (1985).
9. Mass. Gen. L. ch. 119, § 23C; Petition of the Department of Social Services to Dispense With Consent to Adoption, 22 Mass. App. Ct. 62, 491 N.E.2d 270 (1986).
10. Smith v. Organization of Foster Families for Equality and Reform, 431 U.S. 816 (1977).
11. 110 CMR 7.101.
12. 110 CMR 7.105.
13. 110 CMR 7.116.
14. 110 CMR 7.117.

5A.14

Adoption

Adoption is a process that permits adults to be legally made the parents of a child born to others. Because adoption requires judicial approval, adults who wish to adopt are carefully screened. MHPs may contribute to this process by providing evaluations of prospective adoptive parents and children and treatment to the adopted children if necessary.

Adoption Requirements

Adoptive Children

Generally, adoptees are children who were under the age of 18 at the time a petition for adoption was filed. Although "child" is used in the statute, the law does not prohibit adoption of a person past the age of minority. Further, there are provisions for a minor to adopt his or her own natural child.[1] No adoption of brother, sister, aunt, or uncle of the whole- or half-blood is permitted. Prebirth contracts are controlled by a statute forbidding surrender of parental rights before a child is 4 days old.[2]

Adoptive Parents

Any adult, whether married, unmarried, or legally separated, may qualify to adopt children.[3] Persons wishing to adopt a child must file a petition in the probate and family court in the county where

---

1. Mass. Gen. L. ch. 210, § 3(a)(1).
2. Mass. Gen. L. ch. 210, § 2.
3. Mass. Gen. L. ch. 210, § 1.

they live.[4] A nonresident may petition the court in the county where the child resides.[5] Jurisdiction for adoption lies with the probate and family court, which will supply the necessary forms for the proceedings. In addition to a petition for adoption, the prospective parents must also file a petition for change of name.[6] Each adopting parent must make available to the court, through a sworn statement, the child's actual or chosen birth date and the adoptive parents' residence in order to change the birth record of the child to be adopted.[7]

The birth mother must consent to the adoption or the child must be made available for adoption by a termination of parental rights proceeding[8] (see Chapter 5A.10). Additionally, a child 12 years of age or older must also give written consent.[9] A biological father of an out-of-wedlock child is entitled to notice if he has filed a parental responsibility claim[10] or has been adjudicated the father.

The Department of Social Services (DSS) performs pre-adoptive investigations to determine the social and family history of all prospective adoptees under 14 years of age. This information must be submitted to the court within 30 days after DSS receives notice of intent to adopt.[11] All court information relative to an adoption is kept confidential.

The court must consider all information about prospective adoptive parents before deciding whether they are appropriate. Proceedings are usually held in the judge's chambers, and no one outside of the family or interested parties is allowed to be present. In addition, the records of adoption proceedings are strictly confidential.[12] If the case is contested, the court will appoint counsel for the child.[13]

An adoptive parent may petition the probate and family court to undo an adoption. Such petitions are rarely granted. The petitioner must show that the adoption was procured by fraud or deceit.[14]

---

4. *Id.*
5. *Id.*
6. Mass. Gen. L. ch. 210, § 6A; Mass. Gen. L. ch. 210, § 12.
7. Mass. Gen. L. ch. 210, § 4.
8. *Id.*
9. *Id.*
10. Mass. Gen. L. ch. 210, § 4A.
11. Mass. Gen. L. ch. 210, § 5A.
12. Mass. Gen. L. ch. 210, § 6.
13. Mass. Gen. L. ch. 210, § 3(b), as amended by St. 1989, ch. 145.
14. Petition for Revocation of a Judgment for Adoption of a Minor, 393 Mass. 556, 471 N.E.2d 1348 (1984).

5A.15

Delinquency and Children in Need of Services

The juvenile courts and the juvenile sessions of the district courts are responsible for hearing complaints about juveniles who are alleged to be delinquent or to be children in need of services (CHINS). MHPs are often involved in evaluating children before and during the dispositional stage.

Delinquency

A child between the ages of 7 and 17 years who commits an act that violates a criminal statute is generally tried as a juvenile. Juvenile courts are considered noncriminal, although the accused has the same right to counsel and to a jury trial as an adult defendant.[1] Juvenile hearings have two significant differences from criminal trials. First, the hearings are closed to the public unless the child is charged with murder.[2] Second, the child's parents are expected to be present.[3]

Cases can be tried before a judge or a jury. A judge may not sentence a juvenile to prison but can commit the child to the Department of Youth Services, which may have jurisdiction until the child is 21 years old.[4] The statutes are otherwise silent on available dispositions for delinquents. A case must be tried as a juvenile case even if the trial begins after the youth's 18th birthday.[5]

---

1. Mass. Gen. L. ch. 119, §§ 54 and 55A.
2. Mass. Gen. L. ch. 119, § 65, as amended by St. 1990, ch. 267, § 4; News-Group Boston v. Commonwealth, 409 Mass. 627, 568 N.E.2d 600 (1991).
3. Mass. Gen. L. ch. 119, § 56.
4. Mass. Gen. L. ch. 119, § 60.
5. Johnson v. Commonwealth, 409 Mass. 712, 568 N.E.2d 785 (1991).

At any stage in the proceedings, a judge may order an evaluation of the juvenile. This evaluation will be conducted by an MHP under the auspices of a court clinic, the Department of Mental Health, or the Department of Youth Services.[6]

CHINS

The juvenile courts and the juvenile sessions of the district courts have jurisdiction over CHINS cases. These cases involve children who are habitually truant, who are runaways, or who persistently disobey the lawful commands of their parents (stubborn children).[7] CHINS proceedings are designed to provide a child necessary remedial services. Cases are begun by a petition, often brought by a parent. Parents frequently seek evaluations by MHPs before filing CHINS petitions. The cases are assigned to a probation officer who can arrange for examination by MHPs or other experts as an aid for the court.[8]

CHINS cases may be heard before a judge or a jury. The child has a right to counsel.[9] If the judge finds that the allegations in the petition are proven beyond a reasonable doubt, the judge may order mental health or social services or placement of the child to ameliorate the situation.[10] DSS is generally involved in providing necessary services.

---

6. Mass. Gen. L. ch. 119, § 68A.
7. Mass. Gen. L. ch. 119, § 39E.
8. *Id.*
9. Mass. Gen. L. ch. 119, § 39F.
10. Mass. Gen. L. ch. 119, § 39G.

5A.16

Competency of Juveniles to Stand Trial

A juvenile must meet the same standards as an adult to stand trial (see Chapter 5D.5).[1] A judge may order a juvenile to be examined by an MHP for 40 days to aid in disposition.[2] Therefore, MHPs may be involved in evaluating juveniles for competence to stand trial.

---

1. Mass. Gen. L. ch. 123, § 15 (b).
2. Mass. Gen. L. ch. 123, § 15 (f).

5A.17

Nonresponsibility Defense

Minors have the right to raise the insanity defense against delinquency charges.[1] The court can order a juvenile evaluated in a mental hospital for 40 days to aid in the disposition of a case. Therefore, MHPs may expect to evaluate juveniles for criminal responsibility. (See Chapter 5D.9.)

---

1. Mass. Gen. L. ch. 123, § 15 (f).

5A.18

Transfer of Juveniles to Stand Trial as Adults

Under certain circumstances, the law allows a minor to be transferred from juvenile court to the adult criminal courts for criminal prosecution. For transfer to be contemplated, the juvenile must be between the ages of 14 and 17 years and be alleged to have committed an offense which if committed by an adult could lead to a state prison sentence.[1] MHPs may be asked to give an opinion about the advisability of transfer.

Transfer Hearing

The transfer hearing is conducted by a judge with all parties represented. During the hearing the court must determine that an offense has been committed and that probable cause exists to believe that the juvenile committed the offense.[2] Based on clear and convincing evidence, the judge must be satisfied that the minor is not amenable to treatment or rehabilitation as a delinquent child through available facilities.[3] When cases are transferred, the juvenile complaints must be dismissed and criminal charges substituted.[4] For first- or second-degree murder cases, there is a rebuttable presumption that the case should be transferred.[5]

---

1. Mass. Gen. L. ch. 119, § 61, as amended by St. 1990, ch. 267, § 3.
2. *Id.*
3. Mass. Gen. L. ch. 119, § 61; Commonwealth v. Matthews, 406 Mass. 380, 548 N.E.2d 843 (1990).
4. Commonwealth v. White, 365 Mass. 301, 311 N.E.2d 543 (1974).
5. Mass. Gen. L. ch. 119, § 61, as amended by St. 1990, ch. 267, § 3.

5A.19

Voluntary Admission and Civil Commitment of Minors

MHPs may be involved in evaluating minors for involuntary civil commitments and in working with minors seeking voluntary commitment.

Voluntary Admission of Minors

Any minor may seek voluntary hospitalization. In addition, parents of persons under 18 years of age may commit their children.[1] Once admitted, a minor must give 3 days' notice before leaving, unless he or she is discharged by the facility. (See Chapter 5E. 3.)

Involuntary Civil Commitment

Children between the ages of 14 and 17 years may be committed under the same procedures and standards as adults (see Chapter 5E.4). There must be a finding that the child is mentally ill and dangerous to self or others or unable to care for him- or herself in the community. MHPs may evaluate minors to determine whether they meet the standards for involuntary hospitalization.[2]

---

1. Mass. Gen. L. ch. 123, § 10.
2. *Id.*

Commitment by Guardians

Parents who are guardians may commit their children if they have specific authorization to do so.[3]

---

3. In re Roe, 383 Mass. 415, 421 N.E.2d 40 (1981).

5A.20

Education for Gifted and Handicapped Children

Massachusetts has a comprehensive program requiring education of special needs children in public schools. MHPs may become involved in this process by evaluating the children, consulting with special education personnel, and recommending placement of children in special classes.

Principles of Special Education

Massachusetts law[1] requires that all children with special needs receive the individualized program they need. Individual education programs, designed to assure each child as much of a mainstream education as possible,[2] are the cornerstone of the state's special education program. Wherever possible, such individualized programs should use regular classrooms. Additional teachers and special classes may be required.[3] Special education includes both permanent and temporary disabilities and all forms of disability whether physical, cerebral, sensory, perceptual, emotional, or intellectual.[4]

---

1. Mass. Gen. L. ch. 71B, § 2; see 102 CMR 7.00 et seq.
2. Mass. Gen. L. ch. 71B, § 3.
3. Mass. Gen. L. ch. 71B, § 2; see 102 CMR 7.00 et seq.
4. Mass. Gen. L. ch. 71B, § 1.

Referral and Special Education Evaluation

To secure special education services, a child must first be evaluated to determine his or her need for it. The parents, teacher, or school may initiate the evaluation by referring the child to the school's special education coordinator for evaluation. The child can also request an evaluation. The special education coordinator at the school must then obtain written consent from a parent. The parent may also have a private evaluation done by comparable professionals outside of the educational system. The school diagnostic personnel may then rely on the outside evaluation in lieu of conducting their own.[5]

The nature of the evaluation depends on the reason for the referral and the type of services sought. All evaluations are conducted by multidisciplinary teams that must include at least one teacher or other specialist with knowledge in the area of the suspected disability. The evaluation must be done in the child's primary language. If it is other than English, the evaluator must either be fluent in the child's primary language and in English, use an interpreter, or use test instruments that do not stress spoken language and are considered valid and reliable performance measures of functioning.[6]

Some classifications require a "complete psychological evaluation," which means that at a minimum, the test battery must include a comprehensive intellectual assessment test. These evaluations may be undertaken only by a licensed psychologist, a licensed or certified school psychologist, or a psychometrist (see Chapter 1.6). The latter two may only administer the psychological evaluation under the direction of a licensed school psychologist.[7]

The various classifications requiring some type of psychological evaluation are:[8]

1. *educable and trainable mentally handicapped,* which requires a complete psychological evaluation. Intelligence tests must not be the exclusive evaluation device;

2. *learning disabled,* which requires a complete psychological evaluation. To be classified as learning disabled, evaluators must find that the child does not achieve commensurately with his or her age and ability levels in oral expression, listening comprehension, written expression, basic reading skill and compre-

---

5. Mass. Gen. L. ch. 71B, § 3; 603 CMR 300.0.
6. 603 CMR 203.0.
7. Mass. Gen. L. ch. 71B, § 3.
8. 603 CMR 322.2.

hension, or mathematics calculation or reasoning and that the low achievement level is at variance with his or her intellectual ability. The discrepancy between ability and achievement must not be primarily the result of a visual, hearing, or motor handicap; mental retardation; emotional disturbance; or an environmental, cultural, or economic disadvantage; and

3. *seriously emotionally handicapped,* which requires a psychological evaluation that must be conducted by a licensed or certified school psychologist, a licensed psychologist, or a licensed psychiatrist.

Evaluation Team Report

The multidisciplinary team[9] must complete a written report that includes:

1. the reason for the referral,
2. the educationally relevant medical findings,
3. the educational history of the child including complete documentation of efforts to educate the child in a regular classroom,
4. a determination whether the child's educational problems are related to or resulting from reasons of educational disadvantage,
5. the developmental history of the child,
6. the types of tests administered to the child and results of the tests,
7. a recommendation of specific goals and instructional objectives based on current levels of performance needs,
8. a current vision and hearing screening, and
9. an educational evaluation.

Placement in a Special Education Program

The evaluation may lead to a recommendation for services.[10] The purpose of the recommendation is to summarize the results of the evaluation, the child's eligibility for special education placement, and the proposed alternative programs such as special classes, separate schooling, and supplementary aids and services. An individ-

---

9. 603 CMR 322.0.
10. *Id.*

ualized education plan will then be developed for the child by the special education teacher and will form the basis by which future progress is measured and adjusted. The plan must include a statement of:

1. the child's present levels of educational performance;
2. annual goals;
3. short-term instructional goals;
4. the specific special education and related services to be provided to the child;
5. the extent to which the child will be able to participate in regular education; and
6. appropriate objective criteria, evaluation procedures, and schedules for determining on at least an annual basis whether instructional objectives are being achieved.

This plan will be reviewed and revised at least once each school year. A re-evaluation must occur at a minimum of every 3 years.

Parental Rights[11]

Parents must be given written notice, in their primary language if not English, of each step in the special evaluation and placement process. One parent must consent not only to the evaluation but also to the placement and any changes in the placement. If either parent disagrees with the school's evaluation, either parent may request an independent evaluation at public expense. The school can then initiate at its discretion an impartial due process hearing for approval of its evaluation. If the school does not initiate such a hearing, it must provide the funds for the independent evaluation. If the final decision of the impartial due process hearing is that the evaluation is appropriate, the parents still have the right to the independent educational evaluation but not at public expense. This evaluation may be used by the parents to attempt to convince the school that its own evaluation is incorrect.

Impartial Due Process Hearing

On the written request of the parents or school, an impartial due process hearing will be held relating to the evaluation, the placement decision, or whether the written notice requirements were

---

11. 603 CMR 325.0.

followed by the school.[12] If the parents request such a hearing, the school must advise them of any free or low-cost legal services available to them.

The hearing is conducted by an impartial hearing officer knowledgeable about the state and federal laws regarding the evaluation, placement, and education of handicapped children. At the hearing the parties have the right to present evidence and cross-examine witnesses, to prohibit the introduction of any evidence that has not been disclosed to them at least 5 days before the hearing, to present expert witnesses, and to be represented by legal counsel and individuals with special knowledge or training on the problems of handicapped children. The parents have the additional right to have the child present and to open the hearing to the public. The hearing officer will then make a decision on the issue in controversy.[13]

The hearing officer's recommended decision is reviewed by the Department of Education's Bureau of Special Education Appeals. A decision of the Bureau of Special Education Appeals may be appealed to the Superior Court.[14]

---

12. 603 CMR 400.0.
13. 603 CMR 402.0.
14. 603 CMR 410.0.

5A.21

Consent, Confidentiality, and Services for Minors

A minor may not consent to medical treatment;[1] however, this rule has major exceptions. First, a facility may treat a minor in emergency situations that endanger the life, limb, or mental well-being of a minor.[2] Second, a minor may consent to medical treatment if he or she is:[3]

1. married, widowed, or divorced;

2. the parent of a child;

3. in the armed forces;

4. pregnant, or believes herself to be; or

5. living apart from parents and managing his or her own affairs.

In addition, there are specific statutes that permit minors to consent to treatment for venereal disease[4] and drug dependency.[5] Minors may not consent to abortion without parental permission or a court order (see Chapter 5A.22).[6]

MHPs who are approached by minors seeking treatment must be aware that parental consent is necessary unless the treatment is for substance abuse, a sexually transmitted disease, or pregnancy testing. Birth control information and devices may be furnished under the statutory authorization for treatment of venereal diseases

---

1. Baird v. Attorney General, 371 Mass. 741, 360 N.E.2d 288 (1977).
2. Mass. Gen. L. ch. 112, § 12F.
3. *Id. See also* Baird v. Attorney General, 371 Mass. 741, 360 N.E.2d 288 (1977); Baird v. Bellotti, 428 F. Supp. 854 (D. Mass. 1978).
4. Mass. Gen. L. ch. 112, § 12F.
5. Mass. Gen. L. ch. 112, § 12E.
6. Mass. Gen. L. ch. 112, § 12S.

or for a young woman who believes herself to be pregnant.[7] Persons who treat minors are required to ensure confidentiality. The law permits disclosure only with the consent of the minor or a court order.[8] Improper release of medical information may subject the MHP to civil liability.[9]

---

7. Mass. Gen. L. ch. 112, §§ 12E and 12F; Baird v. Attorney General, 371 Mass. 741, 360 N.E.2d 288 (1977).
8. Mass. Gen. L. ch. 112, § 12F.
9. Alberts v. Devine, 395 Mass. 59, 479 N.E.2d 113 (1985).

5A.22

Consent for Abortion

While it is constitutionally forbidden for the state to impose regulations giving parents a veto power over a minor woman's right to an abortion, the state may impose a notification requirement. Massachusetts has enacted such a law that has been upheld by the U.S. Supreme Court.[1] MHPs may become involved in this process by evaluating and testifying as to whether a minor woman is mature enough to decide to have an abortion without parental notification.[2]

Parental Notification Law

The law states that a physician cannot perform an abortion on an unmarried or unemancipated minor woman unless her parents or her legal guardian (or one parent if the parents are divorced) is first notified that she intends to obtain an abortion and gives written consent.[3]

If an unmarried woman who is not 18 years of age does not want to request consent from her parents, she must petition the superior court for approval. A judge will hold a speedy informal hearing in chambers. The judge is asked to determine either (a) that the woman is sufficiently mature to give consent or (b) that it is in the interest of the woman to have the abortion.[4] If the judge

---

1. Mass. Gen. L. ch. 112, § 12S; Bellotti v. Baird, 443 U.S. 622 (1979).
2. *See* Hodgson v. Minnesota, 110 S. Ct. 2926 (1990); Ohio v. Akron Center for Reproductive Health, 110 S. Ct. 2972 (1990).
3. Mass. Gen. L. ch. 112, § 12S.
4. *Id. See also* Matter of Moe, 18 Mass. App. Ct. 727, 469 N.E.2d 1312 (1984).

makes either of these findings, the abortion must be permitted.[5] The judge cannot require that parents be notified.[6] Further, if the judge determines that the minor is mature, then her best interests are never considered.[7] These proceedings are confidential and held quickly, and counsel is appointed for the woman if requested.[8]

---

5. Matter of Moe, 12 Mass. App. Ct. 298, 423 N.E.2d. 1038 (1981).
6. Planned Parenthood League of Massachusetts v. Bellotti, 608 F. Suppl. 800 (D. Mass. 1985).
7. Matter of Moe, 26 Mass. App. Ct. 915, 523 N.E.2d 794 (1988).
8. *Id.*

5A.23

Evaluation and Treatment of Children at the Request of a Noncustodial Parent

MHPs may be asked to provide services to children at the request of noncustodial parents. Massachusetts law[1] provides that where one parent has custody, that person exercises exclusive authority concerning the care and upbringing of the child. The noncustodial parent does not have authority to give legal consent to evaluation or treatment decisions regarding the child. However, in the era of joint custody, it is rare that one parent has such exclusive authority.

Thus, MHPs who provide services at the request of a noncustodial parent without first obtaining the permission of the custodial parent are potentially vulnerable to a malpractice claim on the basis that consent to the services was not given (see Chapter 6.1). This would not apply to situations constituting an emergency or for those treatments for which the minor can consent directly (see Chapter 5A.21). In all other circumstances, MHPs should ensure that divorce and separation decrees and agreements permit the noncustodial parent to request and be responsible for the treatment.

---

1. Mass. Gen. L. ch. 208, § 31, as amended by St. 1989, ch. 689.

Other Civil Matters

5B.1

Mental Status of Licensed Professionals

Professional licensure requirements may consider the mental status of applicants. MHPs may be asked to evaluate a professional's mental status and its effect on job performance and to testify before a credentialing board or a court.

Attorneys

Attorneys in Massachusetts are licensed by the state supreme court. Applicants must demonstrate that they are of *good moral character,* a term that is not defined.[1] There is no specific reference to mental disability.

Dentists

Massachusetts law does not specifically list mental disability as a basis for discipline of dentists.[2] Good moral character is a licensure requirement.[3]

---

1. Supreme Judicial Court R. 3.01.
2. Mass. Gen. L. ch. 112, § 44.
3. 234 CMR 2.01 (20) (a) (2).

Pharmacists

Pharmacists may face disciplinary action if they are found to be physically or morally unfit.[4] Mental illness is not specifically mentioned in licensing requirements.

Physical Therapists

Physical therapists must also meet a standard of good moral conduct to be licensed.[5] Mental illness is not specifically mentioned.

Physicians

Applicants for a medical license and physicians already licensed must possess the mental capability necessary to practice medicine. Physicians may lose their license for a history of mental instability.[6] The Board of Registration in Medicine can order a physician believed to be impaired by reason of mental[7] or physical disability to be examined. The Board can seek a court order to force a physician to undergo the examination,[8] and the results of the examination can be used in disciplinary proceedings.[9]

Psychologists

Psychologists must meet a standard of moral fitness for licensure.[10] Mental disability is not specifically mentioned in the licensing requirements.

Social Workers

The statute on licensure of social workers states that discipline may be imposed after conviction of a crime involving moral turpitude.[11] There is no specific reference in the statute to mental health issues.

---

4. Mass. Gen. L. ch. 112, § 24A; *see also* 247 CMR 7.00 *et seq.*
5. Mass. Gen. L. ch. 112, § 23B; *see generally* 259 CMR 5.04.
6. Mass. Gen. L. ch. 112, § 5.
7. Mass. Gen. L. ch. 112, § 5H; 243 CMR 1.03 (5) (a) (4).
8. Mass. Gen. L. ch. 112, § 5H.
9. *Id.*
10. Mass. Gen. L. ch. 112, § 119.
11. Mass. Gen. L. ch. 112, § 137.

Workers' Compensation

Workers' compensation law[1] provides employees with protection against treatment costs and income losses resulting from work-related accidents or diseases. Employers are required to purchase compensation insurance (or to be self-insured) to provide benefits for injured employees. These benefits are awarded regardless of whether the employee or the employer is at fault. The purpose of the law is to remove work-related injury litigation from the normal court process.

Scope of the Coverage

Workers' compensation benefits are payable for accidents or diseases arising out of or in the course of employment. Compensable injuries include both physical and emotional injuries but do not include mental or emotional injuries resulting from job-related decisions such as firing or demotion.[2]

Workers' Compensation and Mental Stress/Disorder

An employee incapacitated by a mental or emotional disorder causally related to specific work-related stress or incidents is entitled

---

1. Mass. Gen. L. ch. 152, § 1.
2. *Id.*

to compensation under the Workmen's Compensation Act.[3] In addition, mental and nervous disorders resulting from physical trauma are compensable under the act.[4]

Processing a Claim

There are three required stages to every workers' compensation claim. First, an employee who has been injured in an accident or who contracts a disease that he or she believes is work-related must report the condition to the employer within 30 days of the injury.[5] The employer must then report the injury to the Department of Industrial Accidents within 5 days of notification. The department has developed forms for this notification. Second, if the claim is uncontested, the insurer must begin payment within 14 days of the claim being filed.[6] Finally, if the claim is contested, the case will be assigned for an informal conciliation conference and later for a more formal hearing.[7]

Workers' Compensation Benefits

Workers' compensation benefits may include medical, disability, and death benefits.[8] Disability payments cover loss of income during recuperation and are classified according to the seriousness of the injury (i.e., whether it results in a total or partial loss of income) and its duration (i.e., whether it is permanent or temporary).[9] It is possible, however, for an injury to result in more than one classification. For instance, although an injury may initially prevent an employee from working (a *temporary total condition*), it may eventually subside, allowing the person to return to work part-time (*permanent partial*).[10] Death benefits cover burial expenses and payments to the employee's dependents.[11]

---

3. Case of Albanese, 378 Mass. 14, 389 N.E.2d 83 (1979).
4. In re McEwen's Case, 369 Mass. 851, 343 N.E.2d 869 (1976).
5. Mass. Gen. L. ch. 152, § 6.
6. Mass. Gen. L. ch. 152, § 7.
7. Mass. Gen. L. ch. 152, § 11.
8. 452 CMR 2.00 *et seq.*
9. 452 CMR 2.04.
10. 452 CMR 2.02.
11. 452 CMR 2.01.

5B.3

Vocational Disability Determinations

The Massachusetts Rehabilitation Commission (MRC) administers a vocational rehabilitation program funded jointly by the state and federal governments. The program is for persons who have physical or mental disabilities that prevent them from obtaining or maintaining employment but who might be able to engage or continue in a gainful occupation if given vocational rehabilitation services. The intent of the statute is to promote the "rehabilitation, employment, and independent living of handicapped persons."[1] MHPs often evaluate persons for eligibility for vocational rehabilitation services.

Eligibility Requirements

Anyone who is 18 years old, is married, is in the armed forces, or is living away from home and is self-supporting may apply for vocational rehabilitation services. A person who does not meet these requirements may also apply if he or she has a parent or guardian co-sign the application.[2] MRC provides services both directly and through purchase of services,[3] and it administers programs of sheltered workshops.[4]

---

1. Mass. Gen. L. ch. 6, § 74.
2. Mass. Gen. L. ch. 6, § 78; 107 CMR 7.00 *et seq.*
3. *Id.*
4. Mass. Gen. L. ch. 6, § 78A.

Psychological and Psychiatric Services

MRC provides a broad array of services to physically and mentally handicapped persons. These include counseling, transportation, employment, training, and other efforts designed for physical and mental restoration.[5] MHPs are often involved in evaluating MRC clients for eligibility for particular programs. Because MRC develops an individualized rehabilitation program for each client,[6] the report of an MHP can be important in tailoring a plan to a particular client.

---

5. Mass. Gen. L. ch. 6, § 77.
6. 107 CMR 11.04.

5B.4

Emotional Distress as a Basis for Civil Liability

In an action for personal injury, a plaintiff may allege emotional injury. MHPs may be asked to evaluate a person claiming to have suffered an emotional injury from some action or inaction of the defendant.

Intentional Infliction of Emotional Distress

Massachusetts has been reluctant to permit recovery for emotional distress. The actions of a defendant must be characterized as extreme and outrageous and either intended to cause emotional distress or carried out with reckless disregard for the near certainty that distress would result from the conduct.[1] The plaintiff must prove that the conduct of the defendant was outrageous and extreme.[2] For example, an employee who was fired because of stealing at work when there was no basis to believe that the employee had stolen anything, has stated a cause of action.[3] The second element involves the intent or knowledge of the defendant. It is a factual determination. The plaintiff must prove that he or she actually experienced severe emotional distress. In the case of intentional torts, proof of physical injury is not necessary.[4]

---

1. George v. Jordan Marsh Co., 359 Mass. 244, 268 N.E.2d 915 (1971).
2. Agis v. Howard Johnson Co., 371 Mass. 140, 355 N.E.2d 315 (1976).
3. Id.
4. Id.

Negligent Infliction of Emotional Distress

The law[5] also provides for protection against negligent infliction of emotional distress. In this type of case, the defendant did not intend to cause injury to the plaintiff but injury resulted from some action or omission on the defendant's part. The law limits this action by requiring that (a) the emotional distress be manifested as a physical injury; (b) there be a close personal relationship, either by blood or other family-type association, where a person was physically injured and the plaintiff claims emotional distress from witnessing the injury; or (c) the plaintiff was placed in danger of immediate physical injury by the defendant's conduct.[6]

To recover for unintentional infliction of emotional distress, the injury must have been a foreseeable consequence of the defendant's actions and there must be a causal connection between the physical and emotional injuries suffered.[7]

Posttraumatic Stress Disorder

Posttraumatic stress disorder, whether resulting from war experiences or severe experiences such as child sexual abuse, can be the basis for civil liability. The Massachusetts courts have recognized posttraumatic stress disorder as a psychiatric diagnosis.[8] Plaintiffs have sought damages for situations such as sexual abuse in a day-care center[9] and rape in a hospital.[10]

---

5. Payton v. Abbott Laboratories, 386 Mass. 540, 437 N.E.2d 171 (1982).
6. *Id.*
7. Miles v. Tabor, 387 Mass. 783, 443 N.E.2d 1302 (1982).
8. Commonwealth v. Mulica, 401 Mass. 812, 520 N.E.2d 134 (1988).
9. Worcester Ins. Co. v. Fells Acre Day School, Inc., 408 Mass. 393, 558 N.E.2d 958 (1990).
10. Copithorne v. Framingham Union Hospital, 401 Mass. 860, 520 N.E.2d 139 (1988).

5B.5

Insanity of Wrongdoers and Civil Liability

In Massachusetts, persons incompetent by reason of mental illness are still liable for personal injuries that they cause.[1] MHPs may be asked to testify on the competence of a party to participate in a lawsuit.

Procedural Rights of Insane Persons

When someone has been declared incompetent and a guardian has been appointed (see Chapter 5A.2), the guardian stands in for the person in court. Sometimes the court will appoint a guardian ad litem to stand in for the incompetent person during the legal proceeding.[2]

---

1. McGuire v. Almy, 297 Mass. 323, 8 N.E.2d 760 (1937).
2. Superintendent of Belchertown State School v. Saikewicz, 373 Mass. 728, 370 N.E.2d 417 (1977); Mass. Gen. L. ch. 201, § 34.

5B.6

Competency to Contract

A person wishing to contract to buy or sell anything of value must have the mental competence to understand the agreement.[1] A person under guardianship is unable to contract because a court has determined the person incompetent. A guardian can void any contracts a ward makes.[2] MHPs may be asked to evaluate persons for competence to contract.

Legal Test of Competency to Contract

The legal test for competency to enter into a contract is whether the person understood and appreciated the agreement.[3] This is an objective standard based on an assessment of the individual at the time the contract was signed. Testimony of an MHP is critical for this determination.

Determination of Competency to Contract

The determination of competency is a factual issue for a judge or jury. Parties attacking the validity of a contract must prove by clear and convincing evidence that the signer of the contract was in-

---

1. Gurnett & Co. v. Poirier, 69 F.2d 733 (1st Cir. 1946).
2. *Id.*
3. White v. White, 346 Mass. 76, 190 N.E.2d 102 (1983).

competent to contract when he or she signed the contract.[4] Prior conduct of a person may be admitted to show a pattern.[5] Although a party may present evidence of long-standing behavior indicating inability to understand the nature and consequences of a contract, the most important consideration is the person's behavior at or around the time the contract was signed.

The Effect of Incompetency

A finding that a party to a contract was incompetent does not necessarily mean that the contract is void. For instance, if the contract was for necessaries (e.g., food and housing), the law implies an obligation on the part of the incompetent person to pay for them.[6] But where the contract was not for necessaries, it will be rescinded if the status quo can be restored.[7] Where the parties cannot be restored to their original positions (e.g., the land has been improved or the money has been spent), the court will allow the contract to stand despite the incompetency if:[8]

1. the person was not previously adjudged incompetent during a guardianship proceeding,

2. the contract was negotiated in good faith,

3. the person had no reason to suspect the other's incompetence, and

4. the price and terms were fair.

4. Commonwealth v. Bird, 17 Mass. App. Ct. 396, 458 N.E.2d 1198 (1984).
5. Mutual Life Insurance Co. v. Hillman, 145 U.S. 285 (1892).
6. Shaw v. Thompson, 33 Mass. 198 (1834).
7. Becton v. U.S., 489 F. Supp. 134 (D. Mass. 1980).
8. Bucklin v. National Shawmut Bank of Boston, 355 Mass. 338, 244 N.E.2d 726 (1969).

5B.7

Competency to Sign a Will

Individuals who make wills or amend existing ones (referred to as testators) must be competent to understand what they are doing and to be free to resist undue influence.[1] A mental health consultation or testimony may be utilized where an MHP treated or evaluated the testator (but see Chapters 4.2 and 4.3 for limitations on the use of such information). Alternatively, an MHP may be asked to give an opinion of the person's mental status at the time he or she signed the will, based on the reports of other witnesses.

Test of Testamentary Capacity

Anyone 18 or more years of age who is of sound mind may make a will in Massachusetts. The test of whether the testator was of *sound mind* at the time the will was signed requires proof that the testator knew the nature and extent of his or her property; understood his or her relationships with persons who have a natural claim to the estate property (i.e., family members) and whose interests are affected by the terms of the will; and understood the consequences of signing the will.[2] The issue of whether the testator had the capacity to know what he or she was doing is one for a court to determine based on evidence of the testator's condition at the time the will was signed. MHP testimony is very valuable in this determination.

---

1. Mahan v. Perkins, 274 Mass. 176, 174 N.E. 275 (1931).
2. Aldrich v. Aldrich, 215 Mass. 164, 102 N.E. 487 (1913).

Proving Testamentary Incapacity

The decedent (a testator who has died) is presumed to have had testamentary capacity.[3] The party who objects to the admission of the will to probate must prove that the decedent was not of sound mind at the signing of the will. The determination of whether the decedent lacked this capacity is a factual issue for the court, and its decision will not be reversed absent significant error.[4] Expert mental health testimony is frequently admitted to argue for or against the capacity of the testator.

Wills are frequently attacked on the grounds that the decedent lacked testamentary capacity and was unduly influenced by an heir to leave all or most of an estate to that heir. Persons challenging a will must establish the incapacity of the testator to successfully challenge the will.[5]

3. Smith v. Smith, 352 Mass. 766, 225 N.E.2d 590 (1984).
4. Id.
5. Duchesneau v. Jaskoviak, 360 Mass. 730, 277 N.E.2d 507 (1971).

Competency to Vote

The right to vote can be denied or revoked based on a person's mental status. MHPs may be asked to evaluate a person in this regard.

Competency to Register

To vote in a state or federal election, a person must first register to vote.[1] At the time of registration, an individual cannot be under guardianship.[2] Persons under guardianship have been declared by a court to be unable to manage their own affairs and have been placed under the guardian's control (see Chapter 5A.2).

It should be noted that the mere fact that a person is retarded or has been admitted to a mental health or mental retardation facility does not disqualify him or her from voting. It is only when a formal guardianship has been instituted that the disqualification occurs.[3]

---

1. Mass. Gen. L. ch. 51, § 36.
2. *Id.*
3. Boyd v. Board of Registrars of Belchertown, 368 Mass. 631, 334 N.E.2d 629 (1975).

5B.9

Competency to Obtain a Driver's License

There is no per se requirement in Massachusetts that a person must demonstrate legal competence in order to receive a driver's license.[1] However, the Registry of Motor Vehicles does inquire about the mental health history of applicants, and questionable cases are sent to a medical advisory board for determination.[2]

---

1. Mass. Gen. L. ch. 90, § 8.
2. Mass. Gen. L. ch. 90, § 8C.

5B.10

Product Liability

Product liability is a term that describes the law of negligence as it applies to manufacturers, repairers, sellers, and suppliers of products. A product liability claim may be based on principles of negligence or warranty or strict tort liability. The central element of these claims is that the product was unreasonably dangerous to the user. MHPs may evaluate plaintiffs for emotional injury caused by a defendant's products.

Elements of a Product Liability Claim

The law provides that a manufacturer, seller, or supplier is subject to liability for physical harm to a user or a user's property if a product is defective at the time of sale or transfer because of negligent manufacture or maintenance or an inherent design defect.[1]

In a product liability case, the jury is asked to evaluate the gravity of the danger posed by the challenged design, the likelihood that the danger would cause injury, and the feasibility and utility of a safer product.[2] The existence of known dangers may create a duty for the manufacturer or seller to warn the user of the dangers presented.[3] In addition, the manufacturer may have breached certain explicit or implied warranties that may give rise to a lawsuit.[4] Massachusetts does not accept the principle of strict liability with

---

1. McLeod v. White Motor Corp., 9 Mass. App. Ct. 132, 399 N.E.2d 890 (1970).
2. Back v. Wickes Corp., 375 Mass. 633, 378 N.E.2d 964 (1978).
3. Haley v. Allied Chemical Corp., 353 Mass. 325, 231 N.E.2d 549 (1967).
4. Mass. Gen. L. ch. 106, §§ 2–316.

regard to manufactured products.[5] Strict liability makes a product manufacturer liable for injuries caused regardless of fault.

Defenses to a Product Liability Claim

There are three basic defenses to a product liability claim. First, the defendant may introduce evidence that the plans or designs for the product or the methods and techniques of manufacturing, inspecting, testing, and labeling the product conformed with the state of the art at the time the product was first sold by the defendant. This evidence may be considered in determining whether the product was defective and unreasonably dangerous. Second, a defendant is not liable for any alterations or modifications to the product made by a person other than the defendant after the product was sold if those modifications were not reasonably foreseeable by the seller and unknown to him or her. Finally, the plaintiff's use of the product must have been reasonably foreseeable and not contrary to any express and adequate instructions or warnings included with the product that the plaintiff should have known about.[6]

---

5. Allen v. Chance Manufacturing Co., 398 Mass. 32, 494 N.E.2d 1324 (1986).
6. Haley v. Allied Chemical Corp., 353 Mass. 325, 231 N.E.2d 549 (1967).

5B.11

Unfair Competition

Business competitors may engage in fierce competition to control a share of the market. There are laws prohibiting unfair or deceptive practices in a broad array of matters.[1] The area of unfair competition of interest to MHPs, particularly psychologists, is a type of marketing that attempts to confuse the consumer into believing that one business' products or services were produced by another. MHPs may be asked to conduct consumer surveys to determine whether the defendant's business practices resulted in such confusion and to testify in court as to their findings.

Legal Test of Unfair and Deceptive Acts

Whether a given act is unfair or deceptive depends on the circumstances of a particular situation.[2] Questions may arise in virtually any business context including employment agreements and sales of goods and services. One aspect of the law involves failure to disclose material facts in a business or consumer transaction.[3] Another involves discriminatory behavior by giving preference to one purchaser over another.[4] Finally, the law protects against fraud and misrepresentation.[5]

---

1. Mass. Gen. L. ch. 93A, § 2.
2. Noyes v. Quincy Mutual Fire Insurance Co., 7 Mass. App. Ct. 723, 389 N.E.2d 1046 (1979).
3. U.S.H. Realty, Inc. v. Texaco, Inc., 757 F.2d 411 (1st Cir. 1985).
4. Goldstein Oil Corp. v. C. K. Smith Co., 20 Mass. App. Ct. 243, 479 N.E.2d 728 (1985).
5. Bump v. Robbins, 24 Mass. App. Ct. 296, 509 N.E.2d 12 (1987).

Trademark Confusion

A trademark is any word, name, symbol, or device that is used by someone to designate his or her goods.[6] It must be affixed to the goods and must not be a common or generic name. Trademarks are usually registered under federal law but may be registered under Massachusetts law.[7] The purpose of registration is to prevent others from using the trademark.

A business name may be a trademark. Massachusetts law provides that a trademark protects the holder from use of a similar name by another business to the confusion of the public.[8] If such confusion exists, the relevant inquiry for the court is whether the name taken by the defendant had previously come to indicate the plaintiff's business.

6. Mass. Gen. L. ch. 110B, § 1.
7. 950 CMR 64.00 *et seq.*
8. Professional Economics, Inc. v. Professional Economic Services, Inc., 12 Mass. App. Ct. 70, 428 N.E.2d 1221 (1981).

Employment Discrimination

The law[1] prohibits employers from engaging in discriminatory employment practices. The law applies to employers who have six or more employees[2] and to professionals who have employees, as well as management consultants who advise employers concerning personnel selection, discharge, and promotion. MHPs, especially psychologists, should be aware of this law as it pertains to industrial consulting and test construction. MHPs may be called on to testify as experts concerning the validity of tests and testing procedures.

Unlawful Employment Practices

The law prohibits an employer from:[3]

1. failing or refusing to hire or discharge persons or otherwise discriminating against them with respect to compensation, terms, conditions, or privileges of employment because of their race, color, religion, sex, sexual preference, age, or national origin;

2. limiting, segregating, or classifying employees or applicants for employment in any way that would deprive or tend to deprive them of employment opportunities or otherwise adversely affect their status as employees because of their race, color, religion, sex, sexual preference, age, or national origin;

---

1. Mass. Gen. L. ch. 151B, § 1.
2. *Id.*
3. Mass. Gen. L. ch. 151B, § 4.

3. making an employment decision based on the handicap of the applicant if the applicant can perform the job;

4. discriminating solely on the basis of mental health history, including admission to a mental health facility if the applicant is mentally competent to perform the job; and

5. discriminating against a former convict who has not been convicted of a misdemeanor for 5 years.

The law,[4] however, specifically allows:

1. discrimination based on religion, sex, age, or national origin where the status is a bona fide occupational qualification reasonably necessary to the normal operation of the employer;

2. different standards of compensation or conditions of employment pursuant to a bona fide seniority or merit system or a system that measures earnings by quantity or quality of production or that is based on employment in different locations, provided that such differences are not the result of an intention to discriminate or used to discriminate; and

3. giving and acting on the results of any professionally developed ability test provided that the test, its administration, and actions based on its results are not designed, intended, or used to discriminate. Massachusetts has also adopted equal rights statutes[5] and civil rights laws[6] that are stronger than federal laws.

---

4. *Id.*
5. Mass. Gen. L. ch. 93, § 102.
6. Mass. Gen. L. ch. 12, §§ 12H–12I.

Civil/Criminal Matters

5C.1

Jury Selection

Jury selection is the process of choosing citizens to decide civil or criminal cases. Attorneys seek to shape a jury by accepting or rejecting certain jurors. MHPs may be involved in this process by conducting pretrial surveys about a particular case or issue or by evaluating jurors based on the results of pretrial surveys or on in-court observations. The observations of an MHP may determine whether an attorney will favor a particular juror or type of jury.[1]

Juror Qualifications

Massachusetts employs a system of jury selection known as *one day or one trial*.[2] Individuals serve for one day or until the completion of one trial.[3] All citizens between the ages of 18 and 70 can be called for jury duty unless they are incapacitated, have been convicted of a felony within the last 7 years, or are living outside of the jurisdiction.[4] There are no persons, other than those just described, who are automatically excused from jury duty.[5]

---

1. *See* W. Hastie *et al.*, INSIDE THE JURY 227 (1983).
2. Mass. Gen. L. ch. 234A, § 1.
3. Mass. Gen. L. ch. 234A, § 2.
4. *Id.*
5. Mass. Gen. L. ch. 234A, § 4.

Criminal Trials

When a Jury is Allowed

A criminal defendant has a right to request a jury trial when charged with any criminal offense where a jail sentence is a possibility.[6] A defendant may waive the right to trial by jury in writing and have the waiver accepted by the judge.[7]

Jury Size

Felony cases tried in the superior court have juries of 12; misdemeanor cases tried in the district court have juries of 6.[8] Jurisdiction over a case depends on whether a state prison sentence is a possibility. Crimes having only a state prison sentence must be tried in the superior court. Crimes having a state prison sentence or a house of correction sentence may be tried in either court. Other crimes must be tried in the district court.[9]

Unanimity Requirements

The jury must reach a unanimous verdict in a criminal case.[10] If a unanimous verdict cannot be reached, the court will declare a mistrial. Unanimity is a requirement for both conviction and acquittal.

Change of Venue

Criminal defendants and the prosecution may request that the judge move the place of the trial to another county within the Commonwealth if the defendant cannot get a fair and impartial trial in the first county.[11] This request is often made when pretrial publicity has made the defendant so notorious that a fair trial is impossible. MHPs may be involved in designing and conducting a survey of potential jurors within a county to determine the level of prejudice or bias toward the defendant.

Voir Dire

Once a determination on venue is made and a panel of potential jurors is chosen, the parties are given limited information about them.[12] The information includes names, addresses, occupations,

---

6. Duncan v. Louisiana, 391 U.S. 143 (1968).
7. Mass. R. Crim. P. 19 (a); Commonwealth v. Hesler, 1 Mass. App. Ct. 850, 302 N.E.2d 927 (1973).
8. Mass. R. Crim. P. 20.
9. Mass. Gen. L. ch. 218, § 26.
10. See Opinion of The Justices, 237 Mass. 591, 130 N.E. 685 (1921).
11. Mass. R. Crim. P. 37(b)(1); Commonwealth v. Kendrick, 404 Mass. 298, 535 N.E.2d 217 (1989).
12. Mass. R. Crim. P. 20.

and ages of the jurors. The court will randomly summon from the potential juror pool assembled that day the number of jurors needed to serve plus a number of alternates.

The judge then initiates the voir dire examination of the potential jurors by identifying the parties and their counsel, briefly outlining the nature of the case, and explaining the purposes of the examination. The judge may ask additional questions about the potential juror's qualifications to serve on this particular case, including questions requested by counsel. In Massachusetts, attorneys are rarely allowed to interview the jury themselves.

The parties may make an unlimited number of *for cause* challenges. These are challenges alleging that potential jurors are unqualified because they are:

1. witnesses in the action,
2. directly or indirectly interested in the matter,
3. related to any of the parties in the case, or
4. biased or prejudiced in favor of or against either of the parties.

In addition, each side may make *peremptory* challenges. These are challenges not based on cause. The number of peremptory challenges allowed to each side is 12 if the offense charged is punishable by death; 6 (for each count or defendant) in all other cases tried in superior court; and 2 in all cases tried in district court.

When attorneys challenge for cause, the judge makes the final decision as to whether the jurors meet the statutory criteria and must be dismissed. The prosecutor then exercises peremptory challenges followed by the defendant. The process continues until a jury of the required number is selected, plus two additional people in the superior court and one in the district court. This jury will hear the case. Just before deliberations begin, alternate jurors are chosen by lot from this group of jurors. The alternates are kept separate from the remainder of the jury unless something prevents a sitting juror from continuing.

Civil Trials

When a Jury is Allowed

Whether a party in a civil suit has the right to a jury trial depends on whether the action is *at law* or *in equity*.[13] The former generally pertains to actions in which the party seeks damages, i.e., monetary compensation. Cases in equity generally seek nonpecuniary, coer-

---

13. Mass. R. Crim. P. 38.

cive relief such as injunctions (where one party seeks to force the other to stop doing something like polluting a river), restitution (where the defendant is ordered to return the injured party to his or her original condition; if this is impossible, then the suit is for damages and is at law), and specific performance of contracts (where the defendant is forced to carry out the terms of the contract).

Jury Size

A jury in a civil case normally consists of 12 people. The parties may agree to a smaller number.[14]

Unanimity Requirement

Whereas criminal trials require unanimous verdicts, civil matters require the concurrence of two-thirds of the jurors.[15]

Change of Venue

A party in a civil suit may request a change in the place of the trial if the trial will not be fair and impartial. However, the trial court does not have to grant the request. The decision is entirely at the court's discretion.[16]

Voir Dire

Jury selection for civil cases is the same as for criminal trials except that there are no peremptory challenges.[17]

---

14. Mass. R. Crim. P. 48.
15. *Id.*
16. Crocker v. Superior Court, 208 Mass. 162, 94 N.E. 369 (1911).
17. Mass. R. Crim. P. 48.

5C.2

Expert Witnesses

MHPs may testify as expert witnesses if they can provide opinion testimony about matters that are not generally known and if this information will assist the judge or jury in deciding a case. MHPs are frequently called to testify as expert witnesses on a wide variety of issues.

Qualifying as an Expert Witness

The court will allow a witness to testify as an expert if he or she has knowledge, skill, experience, training, or education regarding a subject that is helpful to the judge or jury.[1] The testimony must be relevant and must assist the judge or jury in their decision-making function.[2]

Form and Content of Testimony

The expert witness' authority comes from his or her training and experience.[3] Unlike a normal witness, an expert witness may testify by stating opinions.[4] These opinions can be based on assumptions about evidence in the absence of personal knowledge as long as the assumptions are related to the evidence introduced at trial.[5]

---

1. Commonwealth v. Harris, 1 Mass. App. Ct. 265, 295 N.E.2d 687 (1973).
2. Commonwealth v. Francis, 390 Mass. 89, 453 N.E.2d 1204 (1983).
3. Gill v. Northshore Radiological Associates, Inc., 10 Mass. App. Ct. 885, 409 N.E.2d 248 (1980).
4. Henderson v. D'Annulfo, 15 Mass. App. Ct. 413, 446 N.E.2d 103 (1983).
5. Meehan, *Expert Testimony*, in J. McNaught and J. H. Flannery, MASSACHUSETTS EVIDENCE: A COURTROOM REFERENCE 14–19 (1988).

Before giving an opinion, an expert witnesses must disclose the factors upon which the expert opinion is based. This is referred to as the *foundation of the opinion.*[6] The expert's opinion or inference may touch on the ultimate legal issue to be decided at trial so long as it assists the trier in understanding the evidence and does not decide the issue for the trier.[7]

MHPs are frequently called as experts. For example, most malpractice cases require expert testimony. Thus, in actions alleging malpractice by an MHP, the testimony of another MHP would normally be required to establish the standard of care and how it was breached.[8] Similarly, competency issues require the expert testimony of MHPs.[9] A new area in which MHPs are testifying is identifying sexual abuse of children.[10]

6. Commonwealth v. Boyd, 367 Mass. 169, 326 N.E.2d 320 (1975).
7. Potter v. John Beane Division of Food Machinery & Chemical Corp., 344 Mass. 420, 182 N.E.2d 834 (1962).
8. Murphy v. Conway, 360 Mass. 746, 277 N.E.2d 681 (1977).
9. Commonwealth v. Amirault, 404 Mass. 221, 535 N.E.2d 193 (1989).
10. Commonwealth v. Dockham, 405 Mass. 618, 542 N.E.2d 591 (1989).

5C.3

Polygraph Evidence

Polygraph evidence is not admissible in Massachusetts courts.[1] MHPs who are licensed polygraph administrators may administer polygraph tests, but the results are not admissible in court.

Other Use of Polygraph Evidence

It is a criminal offense for an employer or potential employer to request that an employee or potential employee take a polygraph test.[2]

---

1. Commonwealth v. Mendes, 406 Mass. 201, 547 N.E.2d 351 (1989).
2. Mass. Gen. L. ch. 149, § 19B.

Competency to Testify

A witness in a civil or criminal trial must have the mental capacity to accurately and reliably testify in court. Whenever there is a reasonable doubt concerning the competency of a witness, the opposing counsel or the court should raise the issue. Witnesses under 10 years of age must be questioned by the court to determine their ability to accurately relate facts and to testify in a truthful manner.[1] MHPs have been asked to aid in the assessment of competency.

Legal Test of Competency to Testify

The legal test for mental competency to testify at trial is whether a person is of sound mind at the time of trial[2] or whether the person is a child under 10 years of age who appears incapable of describing accurate impressions of the facts or of relating the facts truthfully. Further, a child must be able to be cross-examined.[3] A history of mental illness can be raised to question the reliability of a witness.[4]

A person's capability to testify is based on his or her capacity at the time of the legal proceeding, not at the time the person witnessed the event in question.[5] Efforts to make it easier for child-victim witnesses by permitting them to testify in criminal trials outside of the presence of defendants have been declared uncon-

---

1. Commonwealth v. Corbett, 26 Mass. App. Ct. 773, 533 N.E.2d 207 (1989).
2. Commonwealth v. Perrault, 13 Mass. App. Ct. 1072, 435 N.E.2d 635 (1982).
3. Commonwealth v. Kirouac, 405 Mass. 557, 542 N.E.2d 270 (1989).
4. Commonwealth v. Gibbons, 378 Mass. 766, 393 N.E.2d 400 (1979).
5. Commonwealth v. Bergstrom, 402 Mass. 534, 524 N.E.2d 366 (1988).

stitutional because of the defendant's right to confront an accuser.[6] Further, children can testify on videotape only if the child and the defendant are both present when the videotaping occurs. A new statute permits out-of-court statements of a child under 10 years of age who has been sexually abused to be admitted into court instead of having the child testify in court.[7] It is unclear whether the statute will be upheld if it is challenged.

Determination of Witness Competency

The determination of whether a witness is competent is not a jury matter but is within the discretion of the judge. The decision-making process may be broken down into three parts, each of which is within the court's sole discretion.[8] First, once a competency issue has been raised, the court determines whether it should conduct a preliminary interrogation of the witness. Second, if there is reasonable doubt about the witness' competency, the court must determine whether to order an additional examination by an MHP. The court may forego a mental status evaluation if it feels that the procedure will not be helpful. Finally, based on its own questioning and any evaluations conducted, the court determines whether the witness is competent.[9] A trial court has broad discretion, and its decision will not be overturned unless there are reasonable grounds to question the court's determination.[10] A court may order a potential witness to be examined by an MHP for competency to testify.[11]

---

6. *Id.*
7. Mass. Gen. L. ch. 233, §§ 81 and 82, added by St. 1990, ch. 339.
8. Commonwealth v. Amirault, 404 Mass. 221, 535 N.E.2d 193 (1989).
9. Commonwealth v. Corbett, 26 Mass. App. Ct. 773, 533 N.E.2d 207 (1989).
10. Commonwealth v. Kirouac, 405 Mass. 557, 540 N.E.2d 270 (1989).
11. Mass. Gen. L. ch. 123, § 19.

5C.5

Psychological Autopsy

Although Massachusetts courts have never used the term *psychological autopsy*, the issue of the mental state of a deceased person is often litigated, particularly in will contests. It is unclear whether Massachusetts courts will allow an analysis of the mental state of the deceased by an expert who had no personal knowledge of the deceased. Generally, testimony by an MHP involves competency determinations made while the person was alive rather than an attempt to reconstruct the competency of a deceased person based on documentary evidence left by the decedent.

Criminal Matters

5D.1

Training and Screening of Police Officers

Some states have statutory requirements for police officers. Massachusetts does not. However, Massachusetts does have a law relating to the training of police officers that includes mental health-related issues. The law does not address, however, whether an MHP has to be involved in such training.[1]

Massachusetts Criminal Justice Training

The Massachusetts Criminal Justice Training Council consists of 24 members appointed by the governor who have experience or education in law enforcement. It includes both public officials and private individuals.[2] Pursuant to statute, the council approves curricula for police training, which must include training relating to rape counseling[3] and domestic violence.[4]

---

1. Mass. Gen. L. ch. 6, § 116.
2. *Id.*
3. Mass. Gen. L. ch. 6, § 118.
4. Mass. Gen. L. ch. 6, § 116A.

5D.2

Competency to Waive the Rights to Silence, Counsel, and a Jury

Persons arrested or questioned by police about a criminal offense they are believed to have committed have the rights to silence and counsel under the United States and Massachusetts Constitutions.[1] MHPs may be asked to examine criminal defendants and to testify as to whether they were competent to waive these rights in the arrest and investigation stages or at the trial. These rights and the right to trial by jury may be waived.

Right to Silence

The right to silence applies as soon as a person becomes the subject of police inquiry. The person must be read a statement of rights that informs them of their right to silence.[2] If an individual is not told of this right, any statements the person makes cannot be used against him or her at trial. After the police read the rights to a person, he or she may waive them and may give any information to the police, including a confession.

In Massachusetts, confessions are assumed to be voluntary.[3] The defendant must raise an issue of involuntariness. In such circumstances, the judge must rule that the defendant was able to understand his or her rights and to make a rational decision. A defendant must be competent to waive the right to silence.[4]

---

1. U.S. Const. amend. V; Mass. Const. part 1, art. 12.
2. Miranda v. Arizona, 384 U.S. 436 (1966); Blaisdell v. Commonwealth, 372 Mass. 753, 364 N.E.2d 191 (1977).
3. Commonwealth v. Tavares, 385 Mass. 140, 430 N.E.2d 1198 (1982).
4. Commonwealth v. Libran, 405 Mass. 634, 543 N.E.2d 85 (1989).

Right to Counsel

A criminal defendant has a constitutional right[5] to be represented by counsel in any criminal proceeding, except those for petty offenses where there is no prospect of imprisonment. Whether the defendant waives the right at trial or at the time of custodial interrogation, the competency test is whether the defendant can make a knowing, intelligent, and voluntary relinquishment of the right. As stated earlier, this determination depends on the particular facts and circumstances of the case, including the background, experience, and conduct of the defendant. Note that the test is not whether an individual has the skill and experience necessary to defend him- or herself. A mentally incompetent defendant cannot waive this right.[6]

Right to Waive a Jury Trial

The test for competency to waive the right to a jury is the same as the test for waiver of the right to counsel.[7] The defendant must be able to make a knowing, intelligent, and voluntary relinquishment of the right. Where there is a substantial question as to the defendant's mental capacity, the court must make an independent determination of whether the person is competent to waive the right.[8]

---

5. Gideon v. Wainright, 372 U.S. 335 (1963).
6. Colorado v. Connelly, 107 S. Ct. 515 (1986); Commonwealth v. Cifizzari, 19 Mass. App. Ct. 981, 474 N.E.2d 1174 (1985).
7. Commonwealth v. Daniels, 366 Mass. 601, 321 N.E.2d 822 (1975).
8. Commonwealth v. Bys, 370 Mass. 350, 348 N.E.2d 431 (1976).

Precharging and Pretrial Evaluations

At any stage of criminal proceedings, a judge can order the defendant examined by one or more "qualified physicians"[1] if the judge is uncertain whether the defendant is competent to stand trial or is not criminally responsible by reason of mental illness or mental defect. This preliminary examination must be conducted, if practicable, at the court house or at the defendant's place of detention.[2] The judge must give instructions to the physician(s) regarding the legal definitions of mental competence to stand trial and for criminal responsibility.

A defendant is presumed competent to stand trial unless either party (defense or prosecution) or the court raises the competency issue. Regardless of who raises the issue, the defendant is entitled to representation by counsel before the court orders an examination. This is because the examination often results in a loss of liberty and, therefore, implicates the constitutional right to counsel, and also because the defendant has a right to be considered for release, with or without bail, despite the need to determine competence.[3]

20- or 40-Day Observational Commitment

If, after the preliminary examination is completed, the judge believes that further examination is necessary to determine whether

---

1. Mass. Gen. L. ch. 123, § 15(a).
2. *Id.*
3. *See* Mass. Gen. L. ch. 123, § 17(c).

the defendant is competent to stand trial or is criminally responsible,[4] the court may order the defendant committed for up to 20 days to a state hospital. Before an observational commitment can be ordered, there must have been a preliminary examination and, if requested by either party, a full hearing, at which the defendant is represented by counsel, on the need for commitment.

Two documents must accompany the defendant to the facility where he or she is committed for further examination or observation. These are:[5]

1. a copy of the criminal complaint or indictment against the defendant, and

2. the report of the physician(s) who conducted the preliminary competency and criminal responsibility examination.

A qualified physician conducting an examination of a defendant during an observational commitment can request an extension of the first observation period if he or she does so, in writing, before the expiration of the initial commitment and specifies the reason why additional time for observation is necessary. On receipt of such a request, the judge may grant an extension, but the total number of days that a defendant can be hospitalized under the first observational commitment and any extension cannot exceed 40.[6] Again, before any extension is granted, the defendant is entitled to a full hearing at which he or she is represented by counsel. There is one exception to this rule: If a criminal defendant on observational commitment requests further hospitalization and the superintendent or medical director of the facility where he or she is committed agrees to provide it, the judge may order further hospitalization there while the criminal charges are pending.

Examining Physician's Report

At the conclusion of the examination period, the examining qualified physician(s) must give the court a written and signed report of findings,[7] "including clinical findings bearing on the issue of competence to stand trial or criminal responsibility." Before examination, the MHP must warn the defendant that he or she has no obligation to say anything and that statements made may be used against him or her.[8] Consequently, unless the defendant is

---

4. Mass. Gen. L. ch. 123, § 15(b).
5. *Id.*
6. *Id.*
7. Mass. Gen. L. ch. 123, § 15(c).
8. Commonwealth v. Lamb, 368 Mass. 491, 334 N.E.2d 28 (1975).

warned that his or her disclosures are not confidential and then knowingly waives the right to remain silent, he or she can prevent their admission into evidence in any subsequent hearing. Reports prepared for competency or criminal responsibility determinations cannot be used for other purposes.[9]

Competency Hearing

If a judge is satisfied, on the basis of the report, that the defendant is competent to stand trial, the criminal proceedings will continue. If the judge believes the defendant is not competent to stand trial, or if the judge wishes to hear more evidence on the issue, the court can schedule a hearing to determine the defendant's competence to stand trial. If the defendant is found incompetent, he or she can be hospitalized.[10] (See Chapter 5D.5.) The court can order a trial stayed until the defendant becomes competent.[11] In addition, during the period of examination, the hospital where the defendant is being held can petition for commitment. A 6-month commitment can be ordered under the same legal standards as civil commitment (see Chapter 5E.4) if the defendant is found incompetent to stand trial (see Chapter 5D.5) or if the charges are dismissed upon commitment.[12]

---

9. Commonwealth v. Blaisdell, 372 Mass. 753, 364 N.E.2d 191 (1977).
10. Mass. Gen. L. ch. 123, § 16 (b).
11. Mass. Gen. L. ch. 123, § 15 (d).
12. Mass. Gen. L. ch. 123, § 16 (b).

5D.4

Bail Determinations

By law, a person charged with a crime has the right to release from jail pending trial on personal recognizance unless the Commonwealth establishes a need for bail.[1] The sole purpose of bail is to ensure that the defendant returns to court when required. MHPs may be asked to evaluate mental condition as it relates to likelihood of flight.

Determining Whether Bail Is Appropriate

Not every crime is bailable. In capital offenses, there is a presumption against bail.[2] The determination as to whether a defendant is bailable must be made at the defendant's first court appearance on the first business day after arrest.[3]

Determining Amount and Conditions of Bail

Once it is determined that the circumstances warrant a bail decision, the court, in its sole discretion, must decide what is the amount of bond, if any, and what are the other conditions of bail. The sole issue in setting bail is whether a bail is required to ensure that the

---

1. Mass. Gen. L. ch. 276, § 58.
2. *Id.* Commisso v. Commonwealth, 369 Mass. 368, 339 N.E.2d 917 (1975).
3. Mass. Gen. L. ch. 276, § 58.

defendant appears in court for trial.[4] In reaching its decision, the court must consider:[5]

1. the nature and circumstances of the offense charged,
2. the weight of the evidence against the accused,
3. family ties,
4. employment,
5. financial resources,
6. character and mental condition,
7. the length of residence in the community,
8. prior criminal record, and
9. record of appearance at prior court proceedings.

As noted earlier, Massachusetts law presumes that no bail is required, and judges who set a bail must explain their reasons for not releasing a defendant on personal recognizance.[6] When a district court sets bail, a defendant is entitled to a bail review in superior court as soon as practicable.[7] Typically, bails in Massachusetts are set in the alternative: a cash bail or a bond of ten times the amount of cash bail.

---

4. *Id.*
5. *Id. See* Commisso v. Commonwealth, 369 Mass. 368, 339 N.E.2d 917 (1975).
6. Mass. Gen. L. ch. 276, § 58.
7. *Id.*

Competency to Stand Trial

To be tried for a criminal offense, a defendant must be aware of and able to participate in any criminal proceedings against him or her. Whenever a judge doubts that a defendant understands the charges, the judge may request an examination for competency to stand trial.[1] MHPs may be asked to conduct the examination.

Legal Determination of Competency to Stand Trial

Test of Competency

Massachusetts has adopted the test established in *Dusky v. United States*,[2] which provides that: "A person shall not be tried, convicted, sentenced, or punished for a public offense while, as a result of a mental illness or defect, he is unable to understand the proceedings against him or to assist in his own defense."[3] There are two elements to this test. First, the person must be suffering from a mental illness or defect. Second, the defendant must be incapable of either understanding the proceedings or assisting in the defense effort.[4]

---

1. Mass. Gen. L. ch. 123, § 15(a).
2. 362 U.S. 402 (1960). Commonwealth v. Blackstone, 19 Mass. App. Ct. 209, 472 N.E.2d 1370 (1985).
3. Commonwealth v. Vailes, 360 Mass. 522, 275 N.E.2d 893 (1971).
4. Commonwealth v. Brown, 386 Mass. 17, 434 N.E.2d 973 (1982).

Competency Hearing

If a judge is satisfied on the basis of MHP testimony that a defendant is competent to stand trial, the criminal proceedings will continue. If the judge believes the defendant is not competent to stand trial or wishes to hear more evidence on the issue, the judge can schedule a hearing to determine the defendant's competence. A finding of incompetency at such a hearing requires a preponderance of the evidence.[5] A *preponderance* means that considering both the quantity and quality of the introduced evidence, more evidence supports a finding of incompetency than a finding of competency.

Either party can request a competency hearing at any time before trial.[6] If a defendant is found incompetent to stand trial, the criminal proceedings against him or her will either be stayed or the charges will be dismissed. If the charges are stayed, the defendant may be committed and tried on the criminal charges if he or she becomes competent at a later date.[7]

Disposition of Defendants Found Incompetent to Stand Trial

Preliminary Observation or Examination

When a defendant is found to be incompetent to stand trial, the court having jurisdiction over the criminal proceedings can order the defendant hospitalized for examination at a state facility. The court-ordered hospitalization can be for up to 40 days, but the total number of days that the defendant is hospitalized cannot exceed 50 days.[8] During this period of observation, or within 60 days after a person is found incompetent to stand trial or not criminally responsible, the district attorney or the superintendent of the facility may petition the court with jurisdiction over the criminal case for commitment of the defendant.

After receipt of such a petition, the court can order the individual committed to a facility for up to 6 months if it makes the findings required for civil commitment[9] (see Chapter 5E.4). While these commitment proceedings are pending, the court can order the defendant temporarily detained at a jail or mental hospital if the period of preliminary observation has expired or if observation was ordered in the first instance.

---

5. Mass. Gen. L. ch. 123, § 15(d).
6. Massachusetts District Court, STANDARDS OF JUDICIAL PRACTICE: CIVIL COMMITMENT 4:01.
7. Mass. Gen. L. ch. 123, § 16 (b).
8. Mass. Gen. L. ch. 123, §§ 15 (b) and 16 (b).
9. Mass. Gen. L. ch. 123, § 16 (b).

The statute also states that if the superintendent, medical director, or district attorney petitions for the commitment of an untried defendant, the petition cannot be heard unless the defendant is first found incompetent to stand trial or the criminal charges are dismissed after commitment.[10] This provision suggests that the petitioners can file a commitment petition against a defendant who has not been found incompetent to stand trial so long as the criminal charges are dismissed if he is committed.

Recommitment Proceedings

After the initial commitment, petitions for further commitment can be filed in the court having jurisdiction over the mental hospital. The court can commit the defendant if it finds that:[11]

1. the requirements for civil commitment are satisfied (see Chapter 5E.4), and

2. the defendant is still incompetent to stand trial (if he or she was committed after a finding of incompetence).

A finding that an untried defendant is now competent to stand trial can result in the defendant being returned to the custody of the original court and in the recommencement of criminal proceedings. For persons who remain incompetent to stand trial or who were competent to stand trial but not criminally responsible, any additional petitions for recommitment (after the first) will be heard by the court having jurisdiction over the facility instead of the court that had jurisdiction over the criminal case.[12]

Notice to the District Attorney

The district attorney for the district where the defendant allegedly committed the crime is entitled to notice of any commitment hearings and has a right to be heard at the hearing.[13] The district attorney has the authority to petition for further commitments.

Court-Ordered Restrictions: Administrative Discharge

Any person committed as incompetent to stand trial can be restricted to the buildings and grounds of the facility by the court that ordered the commitment. These restrictions cannot be removed without court approval or acquiescence. The superintendent of the facility can remove or modify these restrictions if he or she notifies

---

10. *Id.*
11. *Id.*
12. Mass. Gen. L. ch. 123, § 16 (c).
13. Mass. Gen. L. ch. 123, § 16 (d).

the court in writing of the intention to do so and the court fails to object, in writing, within 14 days.[14]

If the superintendent intends to discharge a person committed, or intends not to petition for recommitment at the expiration of a commitment period, he or she must notify the court and the district attorney who had jurisdiction over the criminal case. The district attorney has 30 days from the day he or she receives this notice to petition for further commitment. During this 30-day period, the person will be held at the facility. (The statute does not say so, but presumably the discharge can be effectuated before 30 days if the district attorney notifies the court and the facility that he or she has no objection and will not be petitioning for commitment.) The court and district attorney are not entitled to notice, and the district attorney is not authorized to file a petition, in cases where the criminal charges have been dismissed.[15]

Dismissal of Criminal Charges Against a Person Incompetent to Stand Trial

The statute requires that the criminal charges against a defendant must be dismissed after one-half of the maximum sentence that the defendant could have received if convicted of the most serious crime charged in court has passed. The court must consider good time and other sentence reduction possibilities.[16]

---

14. Mass. Gen. L. ch. 123, § 16 (e).
15. Mass. Gen. L. ch. 123, § 16 (f).
16. *Id.*

5D.6

Provocation

Although provocation is not a justification for the commission of a crime, it can reduce the degree of the offense.[1] For example, a sudden intense passion may reduce a charge from murder to manslaughter because, the court reasons, the crime is without malice.[2] Provocation is not an element of manslaughter but rather provides a defense to murder.[3] Unlike other states, Massachusetts does not permit mere words to constitute adequate provocation.[4] Rather, "passion" or "heat of blood" is required.[5] A gesture indicating a threat of harm may create a defense of self-defense.[6]

1. J. Nolan & B. Henry, CRIMINAL LAW 148–49 (2d ed. 1988).
2. Commonwealth v. Webster, 59 Mass. (5 Cush.) 295 (1850).
3. Id.
4. J. Nolan & B. Henry, CRIMINAL LAW 148–49 (2d ed. 1988).
5. Id.
6. Id.

5D.7

Mens Rea

Most crimes require a specific intent to commit the acts that violate the law.[1] In most cases, a culpable mental state, or *mens rea*, is required to prevent prosecution resulting from inadvertence or accident.[2] MHPs who qualify as experts (see Chapter 5C.2) may give opinion testimony on the question of culpability.

Culpable Mental States

In addition to mens rea, many statutes also require *scienter*, or knowledge of guilt.[3] There are four types of criminal behavior: The most obvious requires a specific intent to commit the criminal act.[4] Crimes such as receipt of stolen property require specific knowledge.[5] Some offenses, such as motor vehicle homicide, require behavior that is so reckless or negligent that guilt is established.[6]

---

1. J. Nolan & B. Henry, CRIMINAL LAW PRACTICE AND PROCEDURE § 644 (2d ed. 1988).
2. *Id.*
3. Commonwealth v. Kelcourse, 404 Mass. 466, 535 N.E.2d 1272 (1989).
4. Commonwealth v. Hawkins, 157 Mass. 551, 32 N.E. 862 (1893).
5. Mass. Gen. L. ch. 266, § 60; Commonwealth v. Boris, 317 Mass. 309, 58 N.E.2d 8 (1944).
6. Mass. Gen. L. ch. 90, § 24 G(b).

5D.8

Diminished Capacity

In some jurisdictions, the law recognizes a defense of *diminished capacity*, also known as diminished responsibility. Under it, defendants assert that although they may have had the requisite mens rea (see Chapter 5D.7), it was severely diminished as a result of a mental disease or defect that should reduce their guilt to one of a lesser offense. In theory, Massachusetts does not recognize this defense. As recently as 1971, the Supreme Judicial Court explicitly rejected it.[1] However, more recent cases suggest that Massachusetts courts may consider evidence that a criminal defendant's mental capacity was impaired.[2] In any cases in which diminished capacity is raised, MHP testimony is critical.

---

1. Commonwealth v. Costa, 360 Mass. 177, 294 N.E.2d 802 (1971).
2. Commonwealth v. Gould, 380 Mass. 672, 405 N.E.2d 927 (1980); Commonwealth v. Grey, 399 Mass. 469, 505 N.E.2d 171 (1987); *See* Greer, *The Rising Tide of Diminished Capacity in Massachusetts*, 1 EXPERT OPINION 1 (Summer 1988).

Criminal Responsibility

An early, yet still controversial, contribution of MHP expertise in the courtroom is in the evaluation of criminal defendants who plead not guilty by reason of insanity because of their mental status at the time of the offense. MHPs may evaluate a defendant and testify as to his or her perceptual and cognitive functioning at the time the criminal behavior occurred. A court may only appoint psychologists and psychiatrists to conduct criminal responsibility evaluations. It is not clear whether a defendant or prosecutor may privately retain other MHPs to conduct the examinations and to testify in court as to their findings.

Legal Determination of Insanity

Massachusetts has long adhered to what is known as the Model Penal Code (or ALI) standard as the test for criminal insanity.[1] The test has two parts:

1. a person is not responsible for criminal conduct if at the time of the conduct, as a result of mental disease or defect, he or she lacks (a) the substantial capacity to appreciate the wrongfulness of his or her conduct or (b) the capacity to conform his or her conduct to the requirements of law; and

2. the term *mental disease or defect* does not include an abnormality manifested only by repeated criminal or otherwise antisocial conduct.

---

1. Commonwealth v. McHoul, 352 Mass. 544, 226 N.E.2d 556 (1967).

Intoxication with alcohol or drugs is not by itself a mental disease or defect that will support a finding of insanity. However, under certain circumstances, an individual's consumption of alcohol or drugs may activate a latent mental disease or defect. Such mental disease or defect may be the basis for a defense of lack of criminal responsibility.[2]

Burden of Proof

Burden of proof of sanity remains with the prosecutor.[3] Insanity is an affirmative defense. A defendant must give notice of his or her intent to use this defense. Once the defendant presents evidence of insanity at trial, the prosecutor must refute the allegation by evidence of sanity.[4]

Mental Examination

A mental examination is key to the insanity defense. A judge may order an examination if there is doubt as to the defendant's sanity at the time the crime was committed, or the defendant may obtain his or her own examination.[5] If the defendant cannot afford an examination and preliminary inquiry indicates that the issue is not frivolous, the court must appoint an MHP to conduct an examination.[6]

Confidentiality and Privileged Communications

In the majority of mental health examinations, the information obtained by psychologists or psychiatrists is confidential (see Chapter 4.2) and privileged (see Chapter 4.3). This is not generally true when a criminal defendant is ordered to undergo a mental status examination. Rather, an MHP must inform a defendant that statements made to the MHP may be reported to the court.[7]

---

2. Commonwealth v. Brennan, 399 Mass. 358, 504 N.E.2d 612 (1983); Commonwealth v. Doucette, 391 Mass. 443, 462 N.E.2d 1084 (1984).
3. Commonwealth v. Soares, 275 Mass. 291, 175 N.E. 491 (1931).
4. Commonwealth v. Jones, 382 Mass. 387, 416 N.E.2d 502 (1981).
5. Mass. Gen. L. ch. 123, § 15.
6. Ake v. Oklahoma, 470 U.S. 68 (1985).
7. In re Lamb, 368 Mass. 491, 334 N.E.2d 28 (1975).

Commitment of Defendants Found Not Guilty by Reason of Insanity

Whenever a court or jury finds a defendant not guilty by reason of insanity, the court will order the defendant held for examination.[8] The standards for commitment to a mental hospital are the same as those for civil commitment (see Chapter 5E.4).[9] A person committed after a plea of not guilty by reason of insanity may spend a longer time in a mental hospital than if he or she had been found guilty and sentenced to prison.[10]

---

8. Mass. Gen. L. ch. 123, § 16.
9. *Id.*
10. Jones v. United States, 463 U.S. 354 (1981).

5D.10

Battered Woman's Syndrome

In some states, the law recognizes battered woman's syndrome as a defense to seriously physically injuring a husband. Massachusetts appellate courts have not specifically approved this defense. However, evidence involving battered woman's syndrome has been admitted into evidence in criminal trials.[1] Because the Supreme Judicial Court has accepted posttraumatic stress disorder as a defense,[2] it is quite possible that battered partner abuse might form the basis for a defense in the future.

MHPs may be asked to provide expert testimony concerning the existence of battered woman's syndrome and the affect of such a syndrome on a person's behavior. Since battered woman's syndrome involves excess force, it may also be the basis for a civil suit for damages. (See Chapter 5B.4).

---

1. Commonwealth v. Moore, 25 Mass. App. Ct. 63, 514 N.E.2d 1342 (1987).
2. Commonwealth v. Mulica, 401 Mass. 812, 520 N.E.2d 134 (1988).

5D.11

Rape Trauma Syndrome

Rape trauma syndrome describes behavioral, somatic, and psychological effects of an attempted or completed rape.[1] In some states the law allows a party to introduce evidence that a rape victim is suffering from rape trauma syndrome to assist in a prosecution where the defendant acknowledges that sexual intercourse occurred but claims that it was consensual; the presence of rape trauma syndrome tends to disprove that the victim consented. It has also been used as a defense when the raped individual attempts to murder the rapist. In this situation, the rape victim attempts to argue that he or she cannot be guilty of the crime since he or she was unable to form the necessary intent to commit that crime because of the syndrome. MHPs may be asked to provide expert testimony concerning the existence of the syndrome and its effect on behavior.

Although Massachusetts law appears to recognize the validity of rape trauma syndrome,[2] it is unclear how the concept will be integrated into the concepts of criminal law.[3] However, as noted in Chapter 5D.10, the acceptance of posttraumatic stress disorder as the basis of a defense suggests that rape trauma syndrome will be accepted in the future.[4] Rape trauma may be a basis for civil liability. (See Chapter 5B.4)

---

1. *See* Commonwealth v. Two Juveniles, 397 Mass. 261, 491 N.E.2d 234 (1986).
2. *See* Mass. Gen. L. ch. 233, § 20J.
3. *Id.*
4. Commonwealth v. Mulica, 401 Mass. 812, 520 N.E.2d 134 (1988).

5D.12

Hypnosis of Witnesses

A person who experienced stress or trauma while witnessing an event may be unable to recount the event in sufficient detail to testify at trial. Hypnosis is a mechanism to help someone recall an event. MHPs may be asked to hypnotize victims or witnesses for this purpose.

Hypnotically Induced Information in a Police Investigation

Hypnotically induced statements may be used as the basis for the issuance of a search warrant only if there is other corroborating evidence.[1] Police must be able to point to some other information that supports what a person said under hypnosis.[2]

Hypnotically Induced Courtroom Testimony

Massachusetts has traditionally held that witnesses in a civil or criminal case who have been hypnotized in the course of investigation or preparation for trial could testify about matters remembered before hypnotism but not those remembered only after hypnotism.[3] While a recent decision of the United States Supreme Court held that hypnotically refreshed witnesses can testify,[4] Mas-

---

1. Commonwealth v. Kater, 388 Mass. 519, 447 N.E.2d 1190 (1983).
2. *Id.*
3. *Id.*
4. Rock v. Arkansas, 483 U.S. 44 (1987).

sachusetts adheres to the rule that testimony of a hypnotically induced witness is limited to prehypnotic memory.[5] Massachusetts has not absolutely excluded all posthypnotic identification, although its use is discouraged.[6]

---

5. Commonwealth v. Kater, 394 Mass. 531, 476 N.E.2d 593 (1985).
6. Commonwealth v. Kater, 409 Mass. 433, 467 N.E.2d 885 (1991).

5D.13

Eyewitness Identification

The role of an eyewitness to an event is critical in many trials. Eyewitnesses may be parties to the action, victims, or bystanders. Their testimony, however, raises the issue of whether their identification at the time of the event, at a subsequent line-up or other identifying procedure, or during the trial is valid. MHPs may occasionally testify about the opportunity of an eyewitness to observe.

Admissibility of Expert Testimony on Eyewitness Identification

Massachusetts law[1] discourages the use of expert testimony to support eyewitness identification. There is a strong preference to have the jury weigh the credibility of the eyewitness. An expert may describe his or her involvement with the eyewitness and can state an opinion about the witness' propensity for truthfulness. However, it is up to the jury, or the judge if there is no jury, to determine how much weight to give the testimony of the MHP.[2]

---

1. Commonwealth v. Peets, 8 Mass. App. Ct. 916, 395 N.E.2d 362 (1979).
2. Commonwealth v. Schulze, 389 Mass. 735, 452 N.E.2d 216 (1983).

5D.14

Competency to Be Sentenced

Although a criminal defendant was found competent to stand trial and criminally responsible, it may, nevertheless, be inappropriate to sentence him or her to a penal institution on a finding of guilty on criminal charges. Massachusetts law allows a judge who wishes to have assistance in sentencing to order the convicted person to submit to a psychiatric examination.[1] An MHP will conduct this initial evaluation at the courthouse.

After this preliminary examination, the judge may commit the convicted person to a mental health facility for a further aid-in-sentencing evaluation for a period not to exceed 40 days. During this observational commitment, the superintendent or medical director of the facility where the convicted person has been sent can petition the court where the criminal trial occurred for civil commitment.

When the examining physician determines that the individual should not be committed, the judge may then proceed to give a correctional sentence.[2] (See Chapter 5E.4.) If the person is not competent, he or she should not be sentenced[3] but committed to a mental health institution until he or she becomes competent to be sentenced.[4]

---

1. Mass. Gen. L. ch. 123, § 15 (e).
2. *Id.*
3. Pate v. Robinson, 383 U.S. 375 (1966); Commonwealth v. Vailes, 360 Mass. 522, 275 N.E.2d 893 (1971).
4. Mass. Gen. L. ch. 123, § 15 (e).

5D.15

Sentencing

After a finding of guilt, the court may request a mental health evaluation before deciding on a sentence.[1] In addition, for serious crimes, a judge will generally delay sentencing until a probation officer can complete a presentencing report. This report details all aspects about the defendant, including mental health history, that may be relevant to sentencing.[2]

---

1. Mass. Gen. L. ch. 123, § 15 (e).
2. Mass. R. Crim. P. 28 (d); Commonwealth v. Martin, 355 Mass. 296, 244 N.E.2d 303 (1969).

5D.16

Probation

A judge may place a defendant on probation following conviction. Probation means that the defendant is under court jurisdiction for a stated amount of time. A defendant placed on supervised probation, where regular reporting to a probation officer is required, must pay a monthly fee to the court or, if the defendant is indigent, perform unpaid community service.[1] In addition, special conditions of probation may be imposed which may include mental health counseling. A court may place an unconvicted defendant on pretrial probation to divert a case from the criminal justice system.[2] Often, mental health or alcohol counseling is a condition of pretrial probation.

Any conduct that violates the terms of probation, even if the conduct does not constitute a violation of criminal statutes, can lead to revocation of probation and, after a probation surrender hearing, to a prison sentence.[3] MHPs may be asked to evaluate persons concerning whether probation is appropriate.

---

1. Mass. Gen. L. ch. 276, § 87A.
2. Mass. Gen. L. ch. 276, § 87.
3. Rubera v. Commonwealth, 371 Mass. 177, 355 N.E.2d 800 (1976).

5D.17

Dangerous Offenders

The criminal sentencing law of some states provides for increasing the term of imprisonment for defendants who pose special risks or who are determined to be dangerous offenders because of a propensity for future criminal activity. In states that have such laws, MHPs are often asked to evaluate defendants for dangerousness. Massachusetts has no similar law.

5D.18

Habitual Offenders

In many states, the criminal sentencing law provides for increasing the imprisonment term of defendants who have a history of criminal offenses. In Massachusetts, an individual who is convicted of a third offense, and the sentence for the previous two offenses was 3 years or more, is supposed to automatically receive the maximum penalty for the third or subsequent conviction.[1] The imposition of a habitual criminal sentence is not affected by MHP testimony. This statute has been upheld against constitutional attacks.[2]

---

1. Mass. Gen. L. ch. 279, § 25.
2. Tuitt v. Fair, 822 F.2d 166 (1st Cir. 1987).

5D.19

Competency to Serve a Sentence

The law in several states provides that a criminal defendant must be competent to serve a sentence. As discussed in Chapter 5D.21, Massachusetts law[1] permits the transfer of mentally ill defendants to mental health facilities in certain circumstances. By inference, therefore, a prisoner must be competent to serve a sentence.[2] MHPs may evaluate inmates for possible transfer to mental health facilities. (See also Chapter 5D.14.)

---

1. Mass. Gen. L. ch. 123, § 18.
2. *Id.*

5D.20

Mental Health Services in Jails and Prisons

Other than as discussed in Chapter 5D.21, Massachusetts law[1] does not address the issue of providing mental health services to incarcerated persons. However, MHPs often provide counseling and other services for inmates (see Chapters 5D.19 and 5D.21).

---

1. Mass. Gen. L. ch. 123, § 18.

5D.21

Transfer From Penal to Mental Health Facilities

When a person in charge of any jail or prison believes a prisoner there is mentally ill and needs to be hospitalized, he or she can order the prisoner to be examined by a qualified physician or physicians at the place of detention.[1] The physician then submits an evaluation on whether or not hospitalization is needed to the district court that has jurisdiction over the place of detention or, if the prisoner is awaiting trial, to the court hearing the criminal case.[2]

Preliminary Examination

The court can then order further examination and observation, for up to 30 days, at a facility or at the Bridgewater State Hospital. Copies of the physician's report completed during this observational commitment are sent to the court and to the person in charge of the prisoner's place of detention. The report must contain "an evaluation, supported by clinical findings, of whether the prisoner is in need of further treatment and care at a facility."[3]

The person in charge of the prisoner's place of detention, the superintendent of the facility where the examination is conducted, or the medical director of the Bridgewater State Hospital can petition the court that received the physician's report for the commitment of the prisoner. After a hearing in which the burden of proof for commitment is the same as that for civil commitment

---

1. Mass. Gen. L. ch. 123, § 18(a), as amended by St. 1990, ch. 272.
2. *Id.*
3. *Id.*

(see Chapter 5E.4), the court may commit the prisoner to a facility.[4] An initial commitment is valid for 6 months. Any subsequent recommitment ordered during the term of the prisoner's sentence is pursuant to civil commitment law and is valid for a 1-year period. (See Chapter 5E.4.) Any prisoner can, with the approval of the person in charge of the place of detention, apply for voluntary admission to a facility.[5]

At the outset of any hospitalization, the Department of Correction must compute the date of expiration of the prisoner/patient's criminal sentence (taking good time and other sentence reduction possibilities into account) and enter that date on his or her hospital record. The prisoner/patient must be discharged on that date unless, prior to the expiration of the sentence, the superintendent of the facility petitions for civil commitment (see Chapter 5E.4).[6] A prisoner/patient hospitalized voluntarily is free to leave the hospital when his or her sentence expires unless the facility successfully petitions for civil commitment.[7]

Return to Original Place of Detention

A prisoner/patient who, prior to the expiration of his or her criminal sentence, is no longer mentally ill and in need of treatment at a facility must be returned to the original place of detention to serve out the balance of his or her sentence.[8]

---

4. *Id.*
5. Mass. Gen. L. ch. 123, § 18(b).
6. Mass. Gen. L. ch. 123, § 18(c).
7. *Id.*
8. Mass. Gen. L. ch. 123, § 18(d).

5D.22

Parole Determinations

Parole is a conditional release from imprisonment that entitles the parolee to serve the remainder of the term outside the confines of the prison.[1] It differs from probation in that the convicted person must first serve a period of time in a prison.[2] While a parole determination is made by the Parole Board, based on information supplied by the Department of Correction, MHPs in or out of the system may be asked to give information at the parole hearing.

Eligibility for Parole

Before inmates may request parole, they must be eligible. Eligibility depends on the type of sentence that was imposed and on the inmate's record while in prison. Generally, a person convicted of offenses involving danger to other persons must serve at least two-thirds of the imposed sentence; most other offenders must serve at least one-third of their sentences.[3]

The Department of Correction evaluates an inmate's record through a parole classification system that classifies inmates according to their criminal history and their record while in prison.[4] This classification process determines whether the Department of Correction supports or opposes parole. MHPs may be used either by the Department of Correction in formulating its recommendations or by the inmate seeking to strengthen the case for parole.

---

1. Mass. Gen. L. ch. 127, § 133.
2. *Id.*
3. *Id.*; Bel v. Chernoff, 390 F. Supp. 1256 (D. Mass. 1975).
4. Mass. Gen. L. ch. 127, § 133A.

Parole Board

The Parole Board consists of five people appointed by the governor who have the appropriate professional or educational qualifications. The board has the exclusive power to pass on and to recommend paroles, reprieves, commutations, and pardons. Its decision is within its sole discretion, which means that a court will not overturn the decision absent a showing that the board exceeded its authority.[5] Reprieves, commutations, and pardons must be granted by the governor, who cannot act without a recommendation from the board.

Parole Criteria

A prisoner who is eligible for parole will be released if the Parole Board is convinced that the prisoner is likely to obey the law after release. The board may impose any conditions on parole that it deems appropriate to ensure that the best interests of the prisoner and the citizens are served. The conditions may include participation in a rehabilitation program or counseling, performance of community service work, and voluntary commitment to the state hospital for a part or all of the parole period. Violation of the terms of parole may lead to reincarceration.[6]

---

5. Petition of Lynch, 379 Mass. 757, 400 N.E.2d 854 (1980).
6. Stefanik v. State Board of Parole, 372 Mass. 726, 363 N.E.2d 1099 (1977).

5D.23

Competency to Be Executed

In states that have the death penalty, the testimony of MHPs is necessary to determine that an individual facing execution is competent. Since Massachusetts has no death penalty and the Massachusetts Supreme Judicial Court has declared the death penalty to be unconstitutional under the state constitution,[1] this section has no relevance under Massachusetts law.

---

1. Commonwealth v. O'Neal, 399 Mass. 242, 339 N.E.2d 676 (1975); Commonwealth v. Colon-Cruz, 393 Mass. 150, 470 N.E.2d 116 (1984).

5D.24

Pornography

The law[1] prohibits any involvement in the preparation, distribution, or sale of obscene books; in selling or displaying obscene materials;[2] or in knowingly giving, lending, showing, or advertising for sale or distribution to minors any explicit sexual material or item that is harmful to them.[3] MHPs who are knowledgeable about the effects of sexually oriented materials may be asked to evaluate and testify on these issues.

As defined by Massachusetts law, obscene means that the average person applying contemporary community standards would find that the item, taken as a whole, appeals to the prurient interest; depicts or describes, in a patently offensive way, sexual activity; and lacks serious literary, artistic, political, or scientific value.[4] Mere nudity itself is not obscene.[5] Massachusetts has both a civil statute for determining that a work is obscene,[6] and a criminal statute making dissemination or possession with intent to disseminate a crime.[7]

---

1. Mass. Gen. L. ch. 272, § 28C.
2. *Id.*
3. Mass. Gen. L. ch. 272, § 29.
4. Mass. Gen. L. ch. 272, § 30D.
5. Commonwealth v. Girard, 358 Mass. 32, 269 N.E.2d 650 (1970).
6. Mass. Gen. L. ch. 272, § 28C.
7. Mass. Gen. L. ch. 272, § 29.

5D.25

Services for Sex Offenders

Under a former Massachusetts law, a person who displayed repetitive or compulsive sexual misconduct and who appeared unable to control sexual impulses could be sent to the treatment center at Bridgewater State Hospital.[1] The treatment center was operated jointly by the Department of Correction and Department of Mental Health. Under this statute, someone was declared to be sexually dangerous after he or she had been convicted of a serious sexual crime, including rape, indecent assault, open and gross conduct, and lewd and lascivious behavior.[2] A judge could request a 10-day evaluation of the person.[3] After the initial evaluation, the judge could commit the individual for a 60-day examination. At the end of the 60-day period, two examiners at the treatment center were required to report to the court. After a full hearing, the judge could declare the person to be sexually dangerous and order him or her committed to the Bridgewater State Hospital for an indefinite time.[4] If the judge found that the individual was not a sexually dangerous person, he or she would impose a regular sentence.

There were two other ways that led to commitment to the treatment center. A prisoner who engaged in sexually assaultive behavior could be transferred to the treatment center from prison if a judge, after a hearing, determined that the prisoner was unable to control sexual impulses;[5] or, a person could apply for voluntary

---

1. Mass. Gen. L. ch. 123A, § 2.
2. Mass. Gen. L. ch. 123A, § 4.
3. *Id.*
4. Mass. Gen. L. ch. 123A, § 5.
5. Commonwealth v. Barboza, 387 Mass. 105, 438 N.E.2d 1064 (1982).

admission if he or she believed him- or herself to be suffering from a mental or physical condition that would likely cause a violation of sex crime statutes.[6]

Court-ordered commitment to the treatment center was for an indefinite time.[7] Each year, individuals committed there could seek court review of their status.[8] In addition, the treatment center established a restrictive integration board to evaluate those committed there for release to community programs.[9] A person was eligible for the program after 2 years at the treatment center.

In 1990, the legislature eliminated the treatment center by repealing all statutory authorization of the provisions for sending individuals there.[10] It is unclear what programs will replace the treatment center.

6. Mass. Gen. L. ch. 123A, § 7.
7. Mass. Gen. L. ch. 123A, § 9.
8. *Id.*
9. Mass. Gen. L. ch. 123A, § 8.
10. St. 1990, ch. 150, § 304, repealing Mass. Gen. L. ch. 123A, §§ 3–7.

5D.26

Services for Victims of Crimes

Victims of violent crime may apply to the courts for limited compensation for loss of earnings as the result of being victimized.[1] In addition, the statewide Victim Assistance Boards and the victim-witness programs in the district attorney offices help victims in putting their lives back in order and in testifying at trial, where appropriate. It should be noted that the law does not mandate a role for MHPs. Victim assistance personnel are generally unlicensed. However, a district attorney is not precluded from retaining an MHP for a counseling function. Also, victims of violent crimes may present statements to a judge for consideration at the sentencing of their assailant. The victim-witness assistance programs aid victims in preparing these statements.[2]

---

1. Mass. Gen. L. ch. 258A.
2. Mass. Gen. L. ch. 258B.

Voluntary or Involuntary Receipt of State Services

5E.1

Medicaid

Medicaid[1] is a federally supported program whereby the states provide direct payments to suppliers of medical care and services for certain eligible individuals. Eligible individuals include those receiving cash payments under the old-age assistance, aid to needy families with dependent children, aid to the blind, and aid to the disabled programs. Other individuals might also be eligible for medical assistance benefits. In Massachusetts the Department of Public Welfare administers this program.[2]

Medicaid eligibility is limited to persons whose assets do not exceed $2,000 for an individual or $3,000 for a married couple.[3]

---

1. 42 U.S.C. 1396 *et. seq.*
2. Mass. Gen. L. ch. 118E; 106 CMR 402.000–462.000
3. 106 CMR 505.110; *See* W. Brisk & W. Tallis, Legal Planning for the Elderly in Massachusetts § 9.3 (1991).

5E.2

Massachusetts Welfare System

Massachusetts provides medical assistance to indigent persons through the Department of Public Welfare.[1] The program covers both inpatient and outpatient mental health services with a preference for community mental health centers operated by the Department of Mental Health or under contract to it.[2] The services are administered via contracts with independent health care providers. Only psychologists and psychiatrists are eligible to provide services.[3]

---

1. Mass. Gen. L. ch. 118A and 118E.
2. *See, e.g.,* Mass. Gen. L. ch. 118A, § 7.
3. *See, e.g.,* 106 CMR 403.000.

5E.3

Voluntary Civil Admission of Mentally Ill Adults

The law[1] provides for the voluntary admission of mentally ill persons to state-operated facilities. MHPs are involved in this process both by evaluating the person for admission and by providing services within the facility.

Voluntary admission may be requested by anyone who is 16 years old, by the parents of someone under age 18, or by a guardian who has the authority to seek admission.[2] Voluntary admission does not mean that a person will be discharged on request. Rather, the patient must file a 3-day notice requesting discharge, and the facility may file a petition for involuntary commitment during that time.[3] The 3-day notice means that a voluntary admission is actually a conditional voluntary admission—conditional on a commitment petition not being filed. Within the 3-day period, the facility may seek to have the person retained by filing a petition for civil commitment. (See Chapter 5E.4.)

---

1. Mass. Gen. L. ch. 123, § 10; 104 CMR 3.03.
2. *Id.*
3. Mass. Gen. L. ch. 123, § 11; 104 CMR 3.04.

5E.4

Involuntary Civil Commitment of Mentally Ill Adults

The law pertaining to involuntary civil commitment concerns mentally ill persons 16 years of age and older. MHPs evaluate individuals for commitment, testify in court as to their findings, and provide services within the facilities where patients are committed. Physicians must be involved in the evaluation process, although other MHPs may assist.

Emergency Commitments

Massachusetts law provides an emergency procedure for involuntarily hospitalization for a person who, if not hospitalized, would create a likelihood of serious harm by reason of alleged mental illness. Emergency hospitalization may not exceed 10 days and may be at a public facility or a private facility approved by the Department of Mental Health.[1]

Procedures

Any physician, qualified psychologist, or "designated physician" may sign an application for a 10-day commitment that sets out their reasons for believing that failure to hospitalize would result in likelihood of serious harm by reason of mental illness.[2] The emergency notice provides the authority to bring an individual to a public mental health facility. In the absence of a doctor, a police

---

1. Mass. Gen. L. ch. 123, § 12; 104 CMR 3.05.
2. 104 CMR 3.07.

officer in an emergency may sign the 10-day application and set forth the basis for commitment. In both instances, the receiving facility will examine the individual and determine whether or not to admit for 10 days.[3]

A third procedure for an emergency commitment is that anyone may apply to a district court judge for a 10-day order.[4] The judge will informally hear reasons for commitment and, if sufficient, can issue a warrant of apprehension to bring the allegedly mentally ill person to court. Following apprehension, the person is examined by a designated physician, and if the physician reports that failure to hospitalize the person would create a likelihood of serious harm by reason of mental illness, the court may order commitment for 10 days.

Procedures for Commitment

Petition for Commitment

The superintendent or medical director of a public or private facility may petition a local district court on an approved form for the commitment of a patient to the facility. The petition must include a factual showing that the person is mentally ill, that the discharge of the person from a facility would create a likelihood of serious harm by reason of mental illness, and that there is no less restrictive alternative for the person. Petitions for commitment to Bridgewater State Hospital must also state that the patient needs strict security that cannot be provided at another facility.[5]

Filing Procedures

Time limits for filing petitions are imposed by statute and must be met by the petitioners in all cases. The petition must be filed in district court before the 3 days have expired in which a voluntary patient has given his or her notice to leave, or before the 10 days have elapsed in an emergency commitment, or before the original commitment has expired in the case of recommitment.

Time Requirements for Hearings

Massachusetts law requires that the hearing on a commitment petition brought under this statute be started within 14 days of the filing of the petition in the district court unless a continuance is requested by the patient or his or her counsel.[6] Since the patient

---

3. *Id.*
4. Mass. Gen. L. ch. 123, § 12(e).
5. Mass. Gen. L. ch. 123, § 8.
6. Mass. Gen. L. ch. 123, § 7(c).

is held at the facility on an involuntary basis pending hearing, it is essential that this provision be complied with. Failure to comply with the 14-day provision constitutes grounds for dismissal of the hospital's petition.[7]

Burden of Proof

Unlike Federal law and the law in most states, Massachusetts requires proof beyond a reasonable doubt for commitment proceedings.[8] The petitioner has the burden of proving in any civil commitment hearing that (a) the patient is mentally ill, (b) the failure to retain the patient in a facility will create a likelihood of serious harm by reason of mental illness, and (c) there is no less restrictive alternative for the patient.

The Department of Mental Health has defined *mental illness* for the purpose of involuntary commitment as a substantial disorder of thought, mood, perception, orientation, or memory that grossly impairs judgment, behavior, capacity to recognize reality, or ability to meet the ordinary demands of life. The definition, however, excludes alcoholism.[9]

Likelihood of serious harm is defined as:[10]

(1) a substantial risk of physical harm to the person himself as manifested by evidence of threats of or attempts at suicide or serious bodily harm;

(2) a substantial risk of physical harm to other persons as manifested by evidence of homicidal or other violent behavior, or evidence that others are placed in reasonable fear of violent behavior or serious physical harm; or

(3) a very substantial risk of physical impairment or injury to the person himself as manifested by evidence that the person's judgment is so affected that he is unable to protect himself in the community and that reasonable provision for his protection is not available in the community.

As a matter of due process, the required finding of dangerousness must be imminent. The petitioner must also establish that the risk of harm is the product of the person's mental illness. Finally, evidence must be presented in every commitment case that there is no less restrictive alternative than hospitalization.

---

7. Hashimi v. Kalil, 388 Mass. 607, 446 N.E.2d 1387 (1983).
8. Superintendent of Worcester State Hospital v. Hagberg, 374 Mass. 271, 372 N.E.2d 242 (1978).
9. 104 CMR 3.01.
10. Mass. Gen. L. ch. 123, § 1.

Decision of the Judge

The judge who has heard the evidence in a contested hearing may order commitment if convinced that the petitioner has proven its case beyond a reasonable doubt or dismiss the petition and discharge the patient. The court must give its decision within 10 days of the completion of the hearing, unless the office of the chief justice of the district court extends the time for an additional 10 days.[11]

Initial commitments are for 6 months, with recommitment for periods of 1 year each.[12] However, a facility may discharge a civilly committed patient on its own initiative at any time during the commitment period.

Medication Order

A petitioner for civil commitment may include a request for medication if the person whose commitment is being sought is refusing psychotropic medication. If the judge first determines that the individual meets the standard for commitment, the petitioner can then ask for a determination of incompetency and a substituted judgment order for medication.[13] (See Chapter 6.2 for a discussion of substituted judgment.)

Appeals

A person who has been committed may appeal alleged errors of law in the commitment proceeding to the Appellate Division of the District Court Department.[14] A person who has been committed may also file a Petition for Discharge to the Superior Court. The person will obtain a hearing before a judge. In such a hearing, the person has the burden of proof to establish that he or she does not meet the criteria for being civilly committed.[15]

---

11. Mass. Gen. L. ch. 123, § 8(c).
12. Mass. Gen. L. ch. 123, § 8(d).
13. Mass. Gen. L. ch. 123, § 8B.
14. Mass. Gen. L. ch. 123, § 9(a).
15. Mass. Gen. L. ch. 123, § 9(b).

5E.5

Voluntary Admission and Involuntary Commitment of Alcoholics

The law provides for voluntary treatment and involuntary commitment of individuals who are seriously disabled by alcoholism, and it alters the focus of the legal intervention from a criminal to a treatment model. MHPs may be part of a multidisciplinary evaluation and treatment team under this law.

Voluntary Admission

An intoxicated person may apply for emergency alcoholism treatment at a local alcoholism reception center. An alcoholic may also apply for evaluation and treatment directly at any treatment facility.[1] Massachusetts law defines an alcoholic as "a person who chronically or habitually consumes alcoholic beverages to the extent that (1) such use substantially injures his health or economic functioning, or (2) he has lost the power of self-control over use of alcohol."[2]

Emergency Admission

Any individual may bring an intoxicated person to a local alcoholism reception center for an emergency evaluation and treatment if that person threatened or attempted to inflict physical harm on

---

1. Mass. Gen. L. ch. 111B, § 2.
2. Mass. Gen. L. ch. 123, § 35, as amended by St. 1989, ch. 352. *See also* 104 CMR 3.07 (4).

him- or herself or on another, or if the person is likely to inflict future harm on him- or herself or on another unless admitted, or if the person is incapacitated by alcohol.[3] Further, a police officer who has reasonable cause to believe a person is intoxicated in a public place and is a danger to one's self or others may use reasonable force to transport the individual to a local alcoholism reception center. If there is no local center or other approved facility, or if the local center is filled to capacity, then the officer may transport the person to a detention facility.[4]

Involuntary Commitment

A police officer, relative, or physician may file a petition for involuntary commitment with a local district court. The petition must allege that the person to be committed is an alcoholic. The court must schedule an immediate hearing and have the individual examined by a physician or psychologist. If the court finds that the person meets the criteria for involuntary commitment, it must order commitment to the alcoholism unit of Bridgewater State Hospital (for men), or Framingham Prison (for women), or an approved private facility for a period not to exceed 30 days.[5]

A person committed under this law may also be discharged before the end of the treatment period if the administrator of the treatment facility determines that the person is no longer incapacitated by alcohol, that treatment at the facility is no longer adequate or appropriate for the person's needs, or that further treatment is unlikely to bring about significant improvement in the person's condition. Treatment may continue beyond the automatic discharge if it is appropriate and the patient agrees.

---

3. Mass. Gen. L. ch. 111B, § 2.
4. *Id.*
5. Mass. Gen. L. ch. 123, § 35.

5E.6

Voluntary Admission and Involuntary Commitment of Drug Addicts

Massachusetts law permits the voluntary admission of drug-dependent persons to facilities for treatment.[1] Substance abusers may also be involuntarily committed. The procedure is exactly the same as that described for alcoholics (see Chapter 5E.5).[2]

---

1. Mass. Gen. L. ch. 111E, § 18.
2. Mass. Gen. L. ch. 123, § 35.

5E.7

Services for Mentally Retarded Persons

The law[1] provides various inpatient and outpatient services to mentally retarded persons through the Department of Mental Retardation. MHPs aid in providing evaluation and treatment services.

As with mentally ill persons, services can be provided on a conditional voluntary basis (see Chapter 5E.3).[2] Individuals residing in state facilities are entitled to an annual review to determine their progress toward discharge.[3] A person who is admitted to a facility for the mentally retarded is not deemed to be incompetent unless a court has appointed a guardian.[4]

---

1. Mass. Gen. L. ch. 123B, § 2; 104 CMR 20.00 *et seq.*
2. Mass. Gen. L. ch. 123B, § 6.
3. Mass. Gen. L. ch. 123B, § 4.
4. Mass. Gen. L. ch. 123B, § 10.

5E.8

Hospice Care

Hospice care is a program of psychological and physical support for terminally ill persons. The program's emphasis is on increasing the quality of someone's last days or months through active participation by the family in caring for the person and through openly facing the meaning and importance of death. There is continued medical assistance in controlling pain and other symptoms to allow the person to concentrate on other aspects of life. A complete program may consist of three phases: (a) home care with nursing, emotional, and religious support; (b) inpatient care with overnight facilities for the family; and (c) bereavement services for the family. MHPs may be involved in all three phases as a member of a support team. Massachusetts has no law relating to hospice care.

Limitations on and Liability for Practice

6.1

Informed Consent
for Services

MHPs should obtain informed consent before administering services, disclosing information about a client to a third party, or taking any other action that impacts on the client. The failure to obtain informed consent renders MHPs liable to a malpractice suit (see Chapter 6.5).

Legal Definition of Informed Consent

It is difficult to determine exactly what constitutes informed consent. A client must give permission for treatment or disclosure, and the permission must be based on sufficient information so that it is given knowledgeably.[1]

For consent to be informed, an MHP must disclose information concerning the nature of the client's problem, the proposed treatment, the benefits and risks associated with the service, the probability of successful outcome, and alternative treatments, if any.[2] This prevents misunderstandings about the nature of the agreement between the MHP and the client. For a client to give informed consent, he or she must be competent to give consent.[3]

---

1. Harnish v. Children's Hospital Medical Center, 387 Mass. 152, 154, 439 N.E.2d 240 (1982).
2. *Id.*
3. Superintendent of Belchertown State School v. Saikewicz, 373 Mass. 728, 370 N.E.2d 417 (1977); *See* Brant, "Last rights: An analysis of refusal and withholding of treatment cases," 46 Mo. L. Rev. 337 (1981).

6.2

Right to Refuse Treatment

It is established law that competent adults have the right to determine whether or not they will receive medical treatment.[1] If a patient is competent, his or her right to accept or refuse treatment is virtually unlimited, even if the patient's decision is difficult to understand.[2] This is not to say that the state maintains no interest in medical decisions. Rather, the state retains four fundamental interests[3]:

1. preservation of life,
2. protection of the interests of innocent third parties (usually minor children),
3. prevention of suicide, and
4. preservation of the ethical integrity of the medical profession.

The state's interest in the preservation of life, standing alone, does not confer absolute power to intervene in private medical decisions. Massachusetts courts have balanced the personal interests of the patient with the state's interest in preserving life.[4] For example, a

---

1. Lane v. Candura, 6 Mass. App. Ct. 376, 377 N.E.2d 1232 (1978); Superintendent of Belchertown State School v. Saikewicz, 373 Mass. 728, 370 N.E.2d 417 (1977); Harnish v. Children's Hospital Medical Center, 387 Mass. 152, 154, 439 N.E.2d 240 (1982); Rogers v. Commissioner of the Department of Mental Health, 390 Mass. 489, 498, 458 N.E.2d 308 (1983).
2. Matter of Spring, 380 Mass. 629, 405 N.E.2d 115 (1980).
3. Superintendent of Belchertown State School v. Saikewicz, 373 Mass. 728, 741, 370 N.E.2d 417, 425–426 (1977); see P. Liacos, "Dilemmas of dying," in Legal and ethical aspects of treating critically and terminally ill patients, 149 (A. E. Doudera and J. D. Peters, Eds., 1982).
4. Superintendent of Belchertown State School v. Saikewicz, 373 Mass. 728, 370 N.E.2d 417 (1977).

competent adult who is a parent of minor children may refuse treatment absent "compelling evidence" that the children would be abandoned because of the death of the parent.[5]

Rights of Children

Parents of young children may not refuse treatment for the children if the medical condition of the child threatens the child's life. The State's interest in protecting children governs.[6]

Rights of Incompetent Patients

While the law is relatively clear concerning competent adults, the legal issues become more complicated with regard to persons who are unable to consent to medical treatment. In such circumstances, other persons must be entrusted with the responsibility for the treatment decision. Massachusetts courts apply a doctrine called *substituted judgment* to make the decision for the incompetent person.[7] Substituted judgment is a subjective analysis of what the individual would choose if he or she could make the election. The court considers detailed aspects about the person—lifestyle, religious interest, as well as prognosis with or without treatment—before making the decision.[8] The first issue is how to determine whether a patient refusing treatment is competent to do so. Competency is always presumed, and the presumption may be overcome only after a guardianship or other legal proceeding.[9]

Health Care Proxies

A new law allows competent persons to designate health care proxies who will be authorized to make treatment or nontreatment

---

5. Norwood Hospital v. Munoz, 409 Mass. 116, 564 N.E.2d 1017 (1991).
6. Custody of a Minor, 375 Mass. 733, 379 N.E.2d 1053 (1978); In re McCauley, 409 Mass. 134, 565 N.E.2d 411 (1991).
7. Rogers v. Commissioner of the Department of Mental Health, 390 Mass. 489, 501 fn. 15, 458 N.E.2d 308 (1983).
8. Superintendent of Belchertown State School v. Saikewicz, 373 Mass. 728, 370 N.E.2d 417 (1977).
9. Matter of Spring, 380 Mass. 629, 405 N.E.2d 115 (1980).

decisions in the event that the person becomes incompetent.[10] Health care providers must follow the instructions of the health care proxy or seek judicial authorization from the Probate and Family Court to override the proxy.[11]

---

10. Mass. Gen. L. ch. 201D, § 1, *et. seq.*, added by St. 1990, ch. 332.
11. Mass. Gen. L. ch. 201D, § 17.

6.3

Regulation of Aversive and Avoidance Conditioning

Although the use of aversive and avoidance conditioning techniques are not regulated in Massachusetts, a recent case illustrates the controversy that this type of treatment may generate. In *Matter of McKnight*,[1] the Supreme Judicial Court reversed a preliminary injunction that ordered Massachusetts to pay for a person's treatment at Behavior Research Institute, a private facility that uses aversive therapies. The state had been seeking to close down the facility. While the Supreme Judicial Court vacated the order for treatment, it did not preclude the use of aversive or avoidance conditioning techniques as appropriate in some circumstances.[2] Aversive treatments therefore remain a possible treatment technique in Massachusetts. MHPs may be asked to consider the appropriateness of aversives for particular clients.

---

1. Matter of McKnight, 405 Mass. 787, 550 N.E.2d 856 (1990).
2. *Id.*

Quality Assurance for Hospital Care

Massachusetts law requires every licensed hospital to organize risk management programs for its medical staff.[1] The law also requires hospitals to organize peer review committees to review the quality of care provided.[2] All proceedings conducted and records and materials prepared in connection with these reviews are confidential and are not subject to discovery by attorneys or admissible in court.[3] They may be obtained, however, for proceedings before the Board of Registration in Medicine and for suits by an individual health care provider against a hospital or its medical staff arising from the latters' refusal to grant privileges or from the termination, suspension, or limitation of the individual's privileges. Hospitals are required to report to the Board of Registration in Medicine any disciplinary action that a hospital takes related to patient-care issues.[4] Hospitals must also report any "major incidents" involving patient care to the board.[5]

The law[6] gives a major role to health care institutions in reporting incidents involving the quality of medical care. In exchange for an ensured confidentiality of peer review proceeding, hospitals are expected to ferret out and report incidents of suspected violations of quality of care standards.[7]

---

1. Mass. Gen. L. ch. 111, § 203(d).
2. *Id.*
3. Mass. Gen. L. ch. 111, §§ 203(a)–(d).
4. Mass. Gen. L. ch. 112, § 53B. *See* Beth Israel Hospital v. Board of Registration in Medicine, 401 Mass. 172, 515 N.E.2d 574 (1987).
5. 243 CMR 3.08.
6. Mass. Gen. L. ch. 111, § 203.
7. *Id.*

6.5

Malpractice Liability

A malpractice suit is a civil action in which the plaintiff alleges that a professional did not exercise the level of ordinary and reasonable care that the average member of the professional's discipline possesses. The law defines medical malpractice as conduct resulting from negligence, error, mistake, or omission that causes injury to a patient.[1] Any person holding himself or herself out as providing professional health services may be sued.[2] This can include MHPs.[3]

Proof of Malpractice

A plaintiff must prove that (a) the defendant-health care provider failed to exercise the same degree of skill and care that is exercised by the average qualified practitioner in the specialty to which he or she belongs acting in the same or similar circumstances, taking into account the advances in the profession and the resources available to the defendant, and (b) the defendant's failure was a proximate cause of the injury.[4]

In a malpractice case, the plaintiff must first establish that a duty of care—a treatment relationship—existed with the defendant.[5] The plaintiff must next establish a violation of the applicable

---

1. Kulas v. Weeber, 20 Mass. App. Ct. 983, 482 N.E.2d 885 (1985).
2. Elwood v. Goodman, 21 Mass. App. Ct. 925, 485 N.E.2d 197 (1985).
3. Leininger v. Franklin Medical Center, 404 Mass. 245, 534 N.E.2d 1151 (1989).
4. McNamara v. Honeyman, 406 Mass. 43, 546 N.E.2d 139 (1989).
5. Stepakoff v. Kantar, 393 Mass. 836, 473 N.E.2d 1131 (1985).

245 MALPRACTICE LIABILITY

standard of care by proving that the defendant's acts or omissions fell below the standard expected of a reasonably prudent member of his or her profession. (The standard of care for MHPs is different for each branch of the profession.) The plaintiff must also show that the acts or omissions of the defendant caused injury to the plaintiff.[6]

Evidence of malpractice must be established by expert testimony, unless it is so grossly apparent that a layperson would have no difficulty recognizing it.[7] Usually, a plaintiff must provide testimony by an expert witness in the same discipline as the defendant's to show what the standard of care is in the same or similar community and that the defendant's actions were not at that level.[8]

The next element of proof of malpractice is proximate cause, a legal term for causation. The defendant's behavior must have caused the injury. The burden is on the plaintiff to introduce evidence that affords a reasonable basis for the conclusion that the defendant's conduct was a foreseeable cause of the plaintiff's injury.[9]

Statute of Limitations

The statute of limitations is the period in which an individual must file a lawsuit. A medical malpractice claim in Massachusetts must be filed within 3 years of the date of injury, or within 3 years of the time that a person knew or should have known facts that would alert him or her to the malpractice claim.[10] If a person is under 18 years of age, of unsound mind, or imprisoned, the 3 year period will not start running until the person becomes 18, becomes sane, or is released from prison.[11] In addition, for sexual abuse of a patient by an MHP, the 3-year period does not begin until the patient knows or reasonably should know that he or she has suffered injury because of the MHP's conduct.[12]

Medical Malpractice Tribunal

Whenever a complaint is filed in superior court alleging medical malpractice, the matter must be referred to a medical malpractice

---

6. DiNozzi v. Lovejoy, 20 Mass. App. Ct. 973, 482 N.E.2d 338 (1985).
7. Delicata v. Bourlesses, 9 Mass. App. Ct. 713, 404 N.E.2d 667 (1980).
8. Kapp v. Ballantine, 380 Mass. 186, 402 N.E.2d 463 (1980).
9. DiNozzi v. Lovejoy, 20 Mass. App. Ct. 973, 482 N.E.2d 338 (1985).
10. Mass. Gen. L. ch. 231, § 60B. *See* Doherty, "The Massachusetts Medical Malpractice Law," 69 MASS. L. REV. 30 (1984).
11. *Id.*
12. Riley v. Presnell, 409 Mass. 239, 565 N.E.2d 780 (1991).

tribunal composed of a judge, a lawyer, and a person in the same discipline as the defendant.[13] Within 15 days from the date that the action was referred to the tribunal, it is supposed to conduct an informal hearing. The tribunal is supposed to assess whether the plaintiff's evidence is sufficient for or a legitimate question for further inquiry.[14] If the tribunal rules for the plaintiff, the case proceeds. If the tribunal rules for the defendant, the case can proceed only if the plaintiff posts a bond.[15] The bond is $6,000 unless reduced by a judge.[16]

---

13. Mass. Gen. L. ch. 231, § 60B.
14. DiNozzi v. Lovejoy, 20 Mass. App. Ct. 973, 482 N.E.2d 338 (1985).
15. Mass. Gen. L. ch. 231, § 60B.
16. *Id. See* Denton v. Beth Israel Hospital, 392 Mass. 273, 465 N.E.2d 779 (1984).

Other Forms of
Professional Liability

In addition to malpractice actions, there are other forms of civil actions that may be brought against MHPs.

Intentional Torts

An intentional tort is a legal wrong involving intended action by a defendant. Intent means that the defendant's conduct did not result from mistake or inadvertence.[1]

Criminal-Related Actions

An MHP may be liable under criminal law (see Chapter 6.7) for actions such as assault and battery and sexual offenses. MHPs may also be liable for the same behavior under civil law.[2]

Defamation of Character

Defamation may either be oral or written.[3] In the former case, it is referred to as slander, while in the latter it is considered a libel. In either form, the injury is to the reputation and good name of a person. This action generally requires that a defendant communicated information (or caused it to be communicated) to a third party that was of such a nature as to harm the plaintiff's reputation. There are two defenses to a defamation suit: (a) the communication was true, or (b) the defendant was privileged (legally entitled) to

---

1. *See* J. Nolan & L. Sartorio, Tort Law 256 (2d ed. 1989).
2. *Id.* at 265.
3. *Id.* at 192.

communicate the information.[4] Privileges may be absolute, such as in a judicial, legislative, or executive proceeding or publication. This means that a witness at a trial or at a legislative committee hearing may not be sued for defamation under any circumstances. Sometimes, a speaker has a qualified privilege, meaning that they are protected from being sued unless the defamatory statements resulted from malice.[5]

Invasion of Privacy

This action involves the communication of private information. It requires proof of a public disclosure of private facts that are not matters of public record or generally known.[6] The disclosure must go beyond an individual or even a small group and be offensive to a reasonable person of ordinary sensibilities. Massachusetts law forbids unreasonable, serious, or substantial invasions of privacy.[7] The release without consent of sensitive private material, such as therapy notes, can constitute an invasion of privacy and subject the person releasing the material to damages.[8]

Other Types of Civil Liability

An MHP may be liable in other types of suits that are based on relationships with clients. An MHP may be civilly liable for breaches of express or implied responsibilities arising out of the MHP–client relationship.[9]

Breach of Fiduciary Duty

The law imposes a *fiduciary duty* on relationships where one party is in a superior position to another with the understanding that the former will act primarily for the latter's benefit. The MHP–client relationship is a fiduciary relationship imposing professional obligations on the MHP not to violate boundaries with the client or reveal confidential information without consent.[10]

---

4. Craig v. Proctor, 229 Mass. 339, 118 N.E.2d 647 (1918).
5. Ramos v. Board of Selectmen of Nantucket, 16 Mass. App. Ct. 308, 450 N.E.2d 1125 (1983).
6. J. Nolan & L. Sartorio, TORT LAW 30 (2d ed. 1989).
7. Mass. Gen. L. ch. 214, § 1B.
8. Tower v. Hirschhorn, 397 Mass. 581, 492 N.E.2d 728 (1986).
9. *Id.*
10. *Id.*

Breach of Contract

Where an MHP contracts to provide services, certain results, or any other tangible or intangible thing that has value in exchange for something of value given by the client (i.e., payment), the MHP will be held liable for breach of contract if he or she fails to live up to his or her part of the bargain.[11] This may involve malpractice if the defendant promised a particular result. For a promise to be enforceable, there must be consideration, i.e., the exchange of something of value for services. Thus, if an MHP guaranteed a result from therapy and the client paid for the therapy, the MHP could be liable in contract for failure to achieve the promised result.[12]

---

11. Goldhor v. Hampshire College, 25 Mass. App. Ct. 716, 521 N.E.2d 1381 (1988).
12. Mass. Gen. L. ch. 93A, § 2; Giannesca v. Everett Aluminum, Inc., 13 Mass. App. Ct. 208, 431 N.E.2d 596 (1982).

6.7

Criminal Liability

Some states have criminal statutes prohibiting MHPs from engaging in certain behaviors, such as sexual relations with a client. Massachusetts does not have such laws, but there are criminal laws that could be relevant to MHPs.

Sexual Offenses

A person commits one of several sexual offenses by engaging in sexual contact (essentially a touching of the sexual parts) or in sexual intercourse (any sort of penetration of the penis, vulva, or anus, or manual masturbatory contact with the penis or vulva) with another without their consent.[1] *Without consent* means that the victim (a) was incapable of consenting because of a mental disorder, age, the use of drugs or alcohol, sleep, or any other similar condition that should have been known to the defendant; (b) was coerced with force or threatened use of force against person or property; or (c) was being intentionally deceived by the offender as to the nature of the act or into erroneously believing that the person was the victim's spouse. An MHP who had sexual contact or intercourse with a mentally disordered person could be found guilty of rape. Nonconsensual sexual contacts other than sexual intercourse are a form of assault and battery.

---

1. Mass. Gen. L. ch. 265, § 13.

Assault and Battery

A person commits assault by either intentionally, knowingly, or recklessly causing any physical injury to another person; by intentionally placing another person in reasonable apprehension of imminent physical injury; or by knowingly touching another person with the intent to injure, insult, or provoke the person.[2] Assaults of a sexual nature are a serious crime in Massachusetts, known as indecent assault and battery.[3]

---

2. *Id.*
3. Mass. Gen. L. ch. 265, §§ 13B and 13H.

6.8

Liability of
Credentialing Boards

Massachusetts law protects individuals who serve on credentialing boards from being sued individually.[1] MHPs registered with the board may sue the credentialing agency to challenge a decision of the entire board.[2]

---

1. Mass. Gen. L. ch. 258B.
2. *See, e.g.,* Morris v. Board of Registration in Medicine, 405 Mass. 103, 539 N.E.2d 50 (1989).

6.9

Antitrust Limitations to Practice

Antitrust laws are enacted to prevent the formation of monopolies and to eliminate abuses of economic power. In recent years, health care providers and their organizations have increasingly become defendants in antitrust litigation. Scrutinized activities include price fixing (an agreement among competitors to establish a common price or system for setting prices), division of markets (an agreement among competitors to allocate certain markets to certain participants), a group boycott (an agreement among competitors to patronize only certain businesses), and tying arrangements (where a party agrees to sell a certain product or service only on the condition that the buyer also purchases a different product). All of these fall under the general prohibition of *restraint of trade*.

The majority of enforcement is through federal law in federal court, but state law also applies. This chapter is limited to Massachusetts antitrust law. It applies to any MHP or organization.

Prohibited Activities

The law is simple in nature; it prohibits restraints of trade.[1] The actions of a Massachusetts health provider in seeking to set fees contrary to the free market may be a restraint of trade.[2]

There are two potential applications of Massachusetts antitrust law to MHPs. First, employment contracts that seek to prevent a

---

1. Mass. Gen. L. ch. 93, § 4.
2. Kartell v. Blue Shield of Massachusetts, Inc., 384 Mass. 409, 425 N.E.2d 313 (1981), 749 F.2d 922 (1st Cir. 1984), *cert. denied,* 471 U.S. 992 (1984).

former employee from practicing after they leave are enforceable if limited in geographic scope and time.[3] Second, exclusive contracts for the provision of mental health services do not generally violate state antitrust laws.[4]

Enforcement of the Law

Any person, or the attorney general, may enforce the law by bringing a lawsuit in superior court requesting equitable relief and damages.[5] The injured party may be reimbursed for reasonable attorney's fees. If the violation is flagrant, up to three times the amount of damages sustained may be awarded. A party must begin an action within 4 years of the date of injury or else it cannot recover any civil penalties.

---

3. Kroeger v. Stop & Shop Companies, 13 Mass. App. Ct. 310, 432 N.E.2d 566 (1982).
4. SDK Medical Computer Services Corp. v. Professional Operating Management Group, Inc., 371 Mass. 117, 354 N.E.2d 852 (1976).
5. Mass. Gen. L. ch. 93, §§ 9 and 12.

Appendix

Table of Cases

Table of Statutes

Table of Rules of Court

Table of Administrative
Rules and Regulations

Table of Other Authorities

Table of Cases

References are to page numbers in this book

Commonwealth v. Moore, 201
Commonwealth v. Mulica, 154, 201, 202
Commonwealth v. O'Neal, 217
Commonwealth v. Peets, 205
Commonwealth v. Perrault, 178
Commonwealth v. Schulze, 205
Commonwealth v. Sheppard, 70
Commonwealth v. Soares, 199
Commonwealth v. Stockhammer, 66
Commonwealth v. Storella, 69
Commonwealth v. Tavares, 184
Commonwealth v. Taylor, 70
Commonwealth v. Truax, 70
Commonwealth v. Tufts, 113
Commonwealth v. Two Juveniles, 63, 67, 202
Commonwealth v. Upton, 70
Commonwealth v. Vailes, 191
Commonwealth v. Varney, 70
Commonwealth v. Webster, 195
Commonwealth v. White, 131
Commonwealth v. Zezima, 68
Copithorne v. Framingham Union Hospital, 154
Craig v. Proctor, 249
Crocker v. Superior Court, 174
Custody of Michel, 114
Custody of a Minor, 117, 124
Custody of a Minor (No. 1), 118
Custody of a Minor (No. 2), 112

D

Delicata v. Bourlesses, 246
Denton v. Beth Israel Hospital, 247
DiNozzi v. Lovejoy, 246, 247
District Attorney v. Board of Selectmen of Sunderland, 33
Doe v. Commissioner of Mental Health, 57
Doe v. Doe, 90
Doe v. Registrar of Motor Vehicles, 77
Duby v. Baron, 47
Duby v. Jordan Hospital, 47
Duchesneau v. Jaskoviak, 159
Duncan v. Louisiana, 172

E

Elwood v. Goodman, 245

F

Fitchburg Housing Authority v. Board of Zoning Appeals of Fitchburg, 48

G

George v. Jordan Marsh Co., 153
Gerstein v. Superintendent Search Screening Committee, 34
Giannesca v. Everett Aluminum, Inc., 250
Gideon v. Wainright, 185
Gill v. Northsore Radiological Associates, Inc., 175
Globe Newspaper Co. v. Boston Retirement Board, 74
Globe Newspaper Co. v. Superior Court, 113
Goldhor v. Hampshire College, 250
Goldstein Oil Corp. v. C. K. Smith Co., 164
Guardianship of Bassett, 89
Guardianship of Weedon, 90
Gurnett & Co. v. Poirier, 156

H

Haley v. Allied Chemical Corp., 162, 163
Harnish v. Children's Hospital Medical Center, 239
Hashimi v. Kalil, 230
Hastings and Sons Publishing Co. v. Treasurer of Lynn, 73
Hellman v. Board of Registration in Medicine, 14
Henderson v. D'Annulfo, 175
Hodgson v. Minnesota, 141

I

In re Adoption of George, 116
In re Lamb, 199
In re McEwen's Case, 150
In re Roe, 90, 133

J

Johnson v. Commonwealth, 127
Jones v. United States, 200

K

Kapp v. Ballantine, 246
Kartell v. Blue Shield of Massachusetts, Inc., 254
Kroeger v. Stop & Shop Companies, 255
Kulas v. Weeber, 245

Superintendent of Worcester State Hospital
  v. Hagberg, 230

T

Tower v. Hirschhorn, 58, 61, 249
Tuitt v. Fair, 210

U

U.S.H. Realty, Inc. v. Texaco, Inc., 164

W

Welch v. Helvering, 54
White v. White, 156
Worcester Ins. Co. v. Fells Acre Day School,
  Inc., 154

Table of Statutes

References are to page numbers in this book

Table of Rules of Court

Rule	Page	Rule	Page
Mass. R. Civ. P. 45	71	Mass. R. Crim. P. 48	174
Mass. R. Crim. P. 19(a)	172	Mass. R. Dom. Rel. P., appendix	99
Mass. R. Crim. P. 20	172	Mass. R. Dom. Rel. P. 35(a)	102
Mass. R. Crim. P. 28(d)	207	Probate Court R. 29B	91
Mass. R. Crim. P. 37(b)(1)	172	Supreme Judicial Court R. 3.01	147
Mass. R. Crim. P. 38	173		

Table of Administrative Rules and Regulations

References are to page numbers in this book

Table of Other Authorities

References are to page numbers in this book

Index

References are to chapters

L

LIABILITY
    Criminal, 6.7
    Malpractice, 6.5
    Other types, 6.6
LICENSURE
    Exceptions/requirements, See each
      profession in Sect. 1

M

MALPRACTICE
    Generally, 6.5
MARRIAGE AND FAMILY THERAPISTS
    Generally, 1.8
MEDICAID
    Generally, 5E.1
MEDICAL ASSISTANCE PROGRAM
    Generally, 5E.2
MEDICAL LIABILITY REVIEW PANEL
    Malpractice action, 6.5
MENS REA
    Generally, 5D.7
MENTAL HEALTH BENEFITS
    State insurance plans, 3.2
MENTAL STATUS
    Of professionals, 5B.1
MENTALLY RETARDED PERSONS
    Services for, 5E.7

N

NARCOTIC ABUSE
    Involuntary treatment of, 5E.6
    By psychiatrist, 1.1
NEGLECT
    Of adults, 5A.7
    Of children, 5A.8, 5A.9
NEGLIGENCE
    Malpractice, 6.5
NURSING
    Licensure, 1.2

O

OPEN MEETING LAWS
    Generally, 1.11

P

PARENT
    Child abuse by, 5A.8
    Termination of rights, 5A.10
PAROLE
    Determinations, 5D.22

PARTNERSHIPS
    Generally, 2.3
PARTY
    In a lawsuit, Editors' Preface
PHARMACISTS
    Mental status, 5B.1
PHYSICAL THERAPISTS
    Mental Status, 5B.1
PHYSICIAN
    Licensure/psychiatrist, 1.1
POLICE OFFICER
    Emergency admission by, 5E.4
    Training and screening, 5D.1
POLYGRAPH
    Evidence, 5C.3
    Examiners, 1.10
PORNOGRAPHY
    Generally, 5D.24
PRECHARGING EVALUATIONS
    Generally, 5D.3
PREFERRED PROVIDER
  ORGANIZATIONS
    Generally, 2.5
PREGNANCY
    Competency to consent to abortion,
      5A.22
PREMEDITATION
    Murder, 5D.7
PRESENTENCE REPORTS
    Generally, 5D.15
PRETRIAL EVALUATIONS
    Generally, 5D.3
PRISON
    Mental health programs, 5D.20
    Transfer to mental health unit, 5D.21
PRIVACY
    Patient/client, 4.2, 4.3
    Records, 4.1, 4.4
PRIVILEGED COMMUNICATIONS
    Generally, 4.3
    Insanity examinations, 5D.9
PROBATION
    Generally, 5D.16
PRODUCT LIABILITY
    Generally, 5B.10
PROFESSIONAL CORPORATIONS
    Generally, 2.2
PROVOCATION
    Generally, 5D.6
PSYCHIATRIC NURSES
    Generally, 1.2
PSYCHIATRISTS
    Generally, 1.1
PSYCHOLOGICAL AUTOPSY
    Generally, 5C.5
PSYCHOLOGISTS
    Generally, 1.3
    School, 1.6
    Subdoctoral and uncertified, 1.4
PUBLIC RECORDS ACT
    Generally, 4.5

R

RAPE TRAUMA SYNDROME
  Testimony, 5D.11
RECORDS
  Confidentiality, 4.2
  Extensiveness, ownership,
    maintenance, access, 4.1
  Privileged communications, 4.3
  Subpoena, 4.4
REGULATION OF
  Aversive conditioning, 6.3
  Hypnotists, 1.9
  Marriage and family therapists, 1.8
  Polygraph examiners, 1.10
  Psychiatric nurses, 1.2
  Psychiatrists, 1.1
  Psychologists, 1.3
  School counselors, 1.7
  School psychologists, 1.6
  Social workers, 1.5
REIMBURSEMENT
  Insurance, 3.1
REPORTS
  Confidential communications, 4.2
  Presentence, 5D.15
  Privileged communications, 4.3
  Search and seizure, 4.4
  Subpoena, 4.4
RESTATEMENT OF THE LAW
  Description, Author's Preface
RULES OF COURT
  Generally, Author's Preface
RULES AND REGULATIONS
  Generally, Author's Preface

S

SCHOOL COUNSELORS
  Generally, 1.7
SCHOOL PSYCHOLOGISTS
  Generally, 1.6
SEARCH AND SEIZURE
  Generally, 4.4
SENTENCING
  Generally, 5D.15
SEX OFFENDERS
  Services for, 5D.25
SEXUAL ABUSE
  Of adults, reporting, 5A.7
  Of children, reporting, 5A.8
  By mental health professionals, 6.5,
    6.7
SOCIAL WORKERS
  Generally, 1.5
SOLE PROPRIETORSHIPS
  Generally, 2.1
SOURCES OF LAW
  Generally, Author's Preface

STATUTORY LAW
  Generally, Author's Preface
SUBDOCTORATE
  Licensure, 1.4
SUBPOENA
  Records, 4.4

T

TAX DEDUCTIONS
  Generally, 3.3
TERMINATION
  Parental rights, 5A.10
TESTATOR
  Competency, 5B.7
TESTIMONY
  Of abused children, 5A.9
  Competency, 5C.4
  Expert witness, 5C.2
TRADEMARK
  Confusion, 5B.11
TRAINING OF POLICE OFFICERS
  Generally, 5D.1
TRANSFER
  Juvenile to adult court, 5A.18
  Prison to mental health facility,
    5D.21
TREATMENT
  Alcoholism, 5E.5
  Commitment of minors, 5A.19
  Involuntary, 5E.4
  Narcotics, 5E.6
  Noncustodial parent requests, 5A.23
  Right to refuse, 6.2
  Voluntary, 5E.3
TRIAL
  Competency to testify, 5C.4
  Expert witnesses, 5C.2
  Privileged communications, 4.3
  Subpoena, 4.4

U

UNCERTIFIED PSYCHOLOGISTS
  Generally, 1.4
UNFAIR COMPETITION
  Generally, 5B.11
UNPROFESSIONAL CONDUCT
  Generally, See each profession in
    Sect. 1
  Liability for, 6.5

V

VICTIMS OF CRIMES
  Services for, 5D.26

About the Author

Jonathan Brant is an attorney in Boston practicing in the firm of Rollins, Moschella, Fowlkes & Brant. The firm concentrates in health and mental health law; administrative law; and civil, domestic, and criminal litigation. Mr. Brant has litigated many mental health cases representing providers, families, and wards.

Although this is his first book, Mr. Brant has published widely on health and mental health topics and is a frequent lecturer to both legal and medical audiences. A graduate of Brandeis University and Harvard Law School, he currently serves as a lecturer in psychiatry at Tufts University School of Medicine. He has been an associate professor of law at New England School of Law, where he taught constitutional law, health law, and mental health law, and a Guberman Fellow in Legal Studies at Brandeis University.

Jonathan Brant serves on the Mental Health Legal Advisors Committee by appointment of the Supreme Judicial Court. He has served on the Governor's Commission on the Unmet Legal Needs of Children, the Task Force on DSS Procedures of the Special Commission on Violence Against Children, and the Children's Hospital Ethics Committee. He lives in Newton, Massachusetts with his wife Renee, a child psychiatrist, and their children Simone and Justin.